Because God Smiled, I am Laughing!

His Grace, the Calling and the Called

Apostle E. Uche Nyeche

authorHOUSE®

AuthorHouse™
1663 Liberty Drive
Bloomington, IN 47403
www.authorhouse.com
Phone: 1-800-839-8640

Edited by Deborah Nyeche and Apostle E.Uche Nyeche

Published by AuthorHouse 4/22/2013

ISBN: 978-1-4817-4560-4 (sc)
ISBN: 978-1-4817-4559-8 (hc)
ISBN: 978-1-4817-4558-1 (e)

Library of Congress Control Number: 2013907435

Dedication

I dedicate this book to the memory of my father late Elder
Israel Wobo Nyeche, you left this world on February 4, 2007.
Dad, ever a hero you were and a mentor to me and many
others. How I wish you lived to see your son today. You
were a true man of faith, and exemplified what a praying
man ought to be. You touched many lives in the community
of Rebisi Port Harcourt, Nigeria and beyond.
You stood tall for righteousness and justice for
all. A tall legacy you have left for me.
Rest in peace and forever in eternal glory,
Apostle Uche

Contents

Special Thanks

Thanks to my Lord and Savior Jesus Christ, You are all that I am.
I give special thanks to my mother Mrs. Eunice Israel Wobo Nyeche.
Mom, I immensely love you for you have been an inspiration. To my
beloved wife Deborah Nyeche, without God using you in my life I do
not know where I would be. May God bless you for all your support
to see that I am all that God has called me to be; you are indeed,
"The Lady."
To my children E. Uche Nyeche Jr. and Adanrundah Nyeche,
your father loves you so much; hope dad has made you guys
proud. To my brothers and sisters Goddy, Dedy, Gloria, Florence
(you know the great work you've done for me) , Promise,
Caroline, Chizi, Anne, and Joy I love you all; and the entirety
of the Nyeche family. To my step-children Danielle and Jamel,
I love you. To my mother-in-law Laura Phelps, thank you for
loving me-I love you, and the rest of the Phelps family.
Special thanks to a special friend Attorney Anthony Molino,
the first contributor to the publication of my book, God
bless you and your heart of generosity. Others who donated
towards the publication of this book, I say thank you.
Now to all those friends over the years who sang the
song of "you need to write because people need to read
your story," you know who you are, and I say thank
you so much for believing in me, this is for you.
May God richly bless every one.
Apostle Uche

Foreword

I affirm that this book is written by someone who has acquired not only the scholarly degrees that satisfy man, but he has experienced the supernatural power of God in ways that many with little faith would find hard to believe. I have had the privilege of observing his response to tragedy, trials, and temptations and he never, and I do mean never, allows it to shake his faith.

Apostle E. Uche Nyeche has an amazing faith like the men of the ancients. He has been called by God and he will not turn back no matter the cost, which thus far has been great. He is a man of vision and character and stands firm on the Word of God. Apostle Uche is a man who prays like a warrior because he knows Satan is a real adversary out to kill and destroy whoever he can. I believe Apostle Uche is the best friend that one can find other than Jesus Christ, because he will not compromise the things of God to win a friend's favor, no matter the prize.

Apostle Uche's experiences with God and His people add a rare dimension to this book as they become a testimony that God is a *living* God. He has written from his experience and by inspiration of the Holy Spirit that he might impact lives around the world. This is a book that can speak to the average person, Christians, pastors, or the scholarly just as well. Apostle Uche has put his heart into this book and I am certainly proud of who he is and what he has shared. I am grateful and not just a little favored by God, to be apart of his life and witness to this endeavor. Glory be to God, *Deborah Nyeche*

Preface

Today is January 29, 2013 at exactly 1:30 am. Wanting to sleep but could not; this writing must begin. For years I have heard from acquaintances the Lord has enriched my life with, friends and co-laborers in faith, who encouraged my writing a book. Their simple phrase collectively has been, "You need to write because people need to read your story. In the years gone by my answer has been that at the appointed time I will commence. I have always enjoyed writing and have known that someday I would begin writing.

The time we live in seems to be an era where everyone is writing a book for various reasons. There have been some wonderful writers who over the years the body of their work has blessed my life. I respect and honor those gifted writers who through their work my life is enhanced. Still this time for me has to come to a full maturity; Let me say that my motivation in writing this book is to bring glory to God.

My whole goal in this life has been nothing but to be known as a serious man who fulfilled the assignment of the work of appellation, in service to God and His people. It is through His grace that I have been *called* to the office of an Apostle. I am constricted with fear and constantly reminded of the weight and awesome responsibility that I carry. It indeed humbles me, and I ask for the prayers of all who read this book, that God's Will be done in my life for His glory; Amen.

Throughout this week the Holy Spirit has stirred up the interest and desire greatly in the writing of this book. As you read I pray you find the blessings of the Living God, gain of wisdom and understanding through my shared experiences. What is the purpose for the book you might ask? It is about the grace of God and how grace is not a license to sin, His *calling*, and the *called*. Additional purpose is to share who God is in my life and for all to know we serve a 'living' God who desires to know us personally. I also aim to dispel those false assumptions with regard to being *called,* verses man-made titles, and the effects of denominations on the church.

I have called this book, "Because God smiled, I am laughing." The reason behind it is that I know Him intimately because He smiled upon me, there is nothing anyone can do to me or say to dissuade me from that knowledge and the relationship I have with my Lord. What I mean when I say He smiled upon me is simple God has told me that I will not make a mistake in this journey with Him so I have full assurance of my assignment with Him. I can laugh because I have a glimpse of the end, I have the victory already, even when people disrespect or disregard me I am not moved because I have a covenant with my God and I have heard directly from my Lord. Of my situation, some would say that this is not how God works. My question often, and in most cases silently is, who can tell me what Is of God?" And at this also I laugh.

Chapter 1

Who am I?

I am U.S. citizen, originally from River State, Nigeria. I was born to great and wonderful parents; late Israel Wobo Nyeche and my mother Eunice Nyeche in a place called Oromeruezimgbu in Rebisi, presently known as Port Harcourt in Nigeria. My elementary and secondary school was in River State. I had a brief work experience with the shipping industry and an oil drilling company until my departure from Nigeria in 1979/80 to Athens, Greece and eventually to the shores of America in the early eighties.

I grew up in Christian family and was baptized at the age ten at St. Paul's Anglican Church under the first name of Victor. Unceremoniously my name was changed from Victor to Evans, for reasons that now make no sense. Since 1971/72 at my family home there has always been early morning observance of praise and worship to God lifted to His holy name. Every one visiting my family knew the routine and if they were for any reason unaware, they knew it after their first night spent. No one left the home or prepared for work or anything before our holy devotion. All that was to commence began after praying and thanking the LORD ALMIGHTY for His goodness and mercy.

It was at these morning devotions that my *calling* was pronounced by a gifted prophet, leaving with me the vivid indelible pronouncement in my early to late teens. Another man gifted of God called prophet Silas was the one who declared this to my parents pointing straight at my face, "Listen, whether you like it or not you have been *called* to do work of the LORD." The full meaning did not immediately register as to its profundity.

I had purposed to become a lawyer, for my father's life on earth was that of a man who believed in justice and righteousness for all and in his stance for justice my father never relented for what was right; whether for personal cause or the community at large. In this itinerary in my father's life courthouse experiences were familiar throughout my family. So, early on I became interested in a law career, even more so my desire was to relieve my father from some of the burden of legal fees.

The hunger for me in life never was becoming a priest; I did not think of myself worthy of being a man of the cloth. I hear people state that they have always wanted to become a pastor, not me. Who I am today was after years of running from serving the Lord and the journey to this point has been indeed a journey, for the proposal of man is not always the disposition of God. Further on in this book I will discuss on the call of God on my life in a much greater detail.

Though I did not complete law school, I hold a Diploma in Greek from the University of Athens, Greece; B.A. in Political Science/Psychology from the University of La Verne, C.A; and more recently a M.A. in Theology and an M.A. in Theology and Ministry, from Fuller Theological Seminary, Pasadena, C.A. Currently I am pursuing a Ph. D. Degree in Public Policy and Administration-Nonprofit Mgmt & Leadership.

Chapter 2

Professional Minister and the Called

I must start by letting the reader know that I am not a *professional minister* neither do I fancy the likes of it, rather I have been *called*-out by God. If this statement makes anyone queasy, I seek no intentional offense but my confession is to the truth. Professional ministers are professional copy masters of the *called* but counterfeit in truth. They may have talents, appear well-dressed, often good talkers of game, but at best they have no spiritual power, and at the worst they are nothing but deceivers of the vulnerable and the faithful. They rise quick to earthly success, even the discerning *called* run the risk of being deceived. What is the difference? The former chooses the industry as a profession and the product is a ministry void of the presence of the Holy Spirit and exaltation of self. They are those who follow commercial trends in the work of the ministry. Every extreme is exercised for the emergence of success and to them it matters.

Some professional ministers follow the footsteps of those who have the appearance of success because they are not God centered they have their own vision and that is to take the easy road. I put no denunciation of their emulation but find it sordid when they use it in the name of God. A great many of these preach nothing but prosperity, and for them God is only in the blessing business, nothing more and nothing less. They would say that if you are poor it's your fault because God has not created you to be poor. Be it further from the truth I deny that God desires what is good for us, be that material or financial prosperity; above all however, I believe that God desires most of all that we live a life that glorifies Him. And, it is also untrue and unbiblical that God has created all to be materially wealthy.

Bear in mind the scripture in Deuteronomy 15:11, "For the poor will never cease to be in the land, therefore I command you, saying,' you shall freely open your hand to your brother, to your needy and poor in the land." And then the words of Jesus in Mark 14:7, "For you always have the poor with you, and whenever you wish you can do good to them; but you do not always have Me." This is what is biblical and true. Other times they are prone to say…., if you fall sick there must be sin in your life or their theological underpinnings may be, "God does not cause sickness." Yet, this also is false for the bible states in John 9: 3, "it was neither that this man sinned, nor his parents; but it was so that the works of God might be displayed in him." These are the teachings of the bible; such instances are clearly stated through out the bible from the Old Testament narrations to the New Testament with the case of Apostle Paul and the torn on his flesh. The kinds of excavations pushed forward by these professional ministers are not biblical rather their teachings are contrary to the words of God.

A lot of the professional ministers are experts in marketing themselves as the kinder and gentler people, yet as conniving as the devil. They claim to understand the felt need of the people but they focus and zoom into the fragile emotions of the weak; while deep down their motives are wrong and intentions fraught with dubiousness. It is because of this that Jesus warns us to be as wise as serpents. They are indeed the ravenous wolves whose furs are woven in sheep's clothing. They preach the gospel of psychology instead of the gospel of Jesus Christ. Their teaching is all about self-help and emotional feelings that are centered on happiness. What is happiness the reader might ask….? Well, let us continue.

We know that happiness of the moment is found in pleasurable contentment and that it does not last through the course of time. This is why Jesus speaks on what is essential and sustaining, which is peace. The Peace of God enables the saints of God to secure peace in troubled times. This Peace can only come through Jesus and is expressed genuinely by those who are *called* and not by the professional ministers who are not called by Jesus nor do they have personal relationship with the LORD. Professional ministers are accurately portrayed iconographical by Jesus as "hired hands" who care nothing about the sheep, they scatter as the wolf approaches… they flee. Saints of God, professional ministers do not have the ardor of Jesus Christ in them.

Most of these ministers are powerless because they are not after God's own heart but material wealth and prominent positions. The bible states in Matthew 6:33, "seeking first His Kingdom and His righteousness, and all these things will be added to you." The professional ministers see it differently. Instead of what Jesus was talking about which was first the salvation that was to come from the heavenly kingdom and with it God's provision, the professional ministers seek their own coveted kingdom of earthly possessions. They see their provision in the material things and not from the Heavenly kingdom. There is a stark difference between these and those who are *called*.

The *called* minister is one whose desire is to please the one who called him or her. The aspiration and goal is to do God's Holy Will. This does not mean that he or she is perfect or holier but that these shepherds seek to be used for the good of God's people, enabling them by His grace to achieve their purpose in life. The *called* of God die to self to please the one who has *called* them, and they measure their desire with the reverential fear of the almighty God. These are people who are purposeful in their fellowship and not platform hungry. They walk in humility and understand what it means to wait. They are long in the obedience of the things of God and frown at disobedient hearts.

The *called* remain aware that the work for which they are *called* is not theirs but the work of God. The *called* understand the danger of running ahead of God, for one could end up in a spiritual wilderness, or worse. The *called* understand that there is suffering and the bible makes no short mentions of that; bluntly put that the entire bible is full of the examples of those before us. The *called* walk in adoration and the heart of holiness, spend time in prayer, hold up their own integrity, truth, honesty, and have no misgiving in knowing that with the blessings of God comes a greater mandate in responsible living and care for the least among us.

The *called* honor God because they know that His true knowledge comes through His grace and that it is only with Him we become who we are called. The *called* are the true shepherds embodied in the Lord as the only good Shepherd. The *called* know whose they are and the Lord knows them by name. The Lord lay down His life, therefore the *called* lay down their life daily through various tribulations and sacrifice to the glory of our Lord and Savior, Jesus Christ.

The *called* in their relationship with the Father is summed up and described by Jesus in John 10: 18, "even as the Father knows Me and I know the Father; and I lay down my life for the sheep." The *called* in their perfunctory quest find the trajectory of feeding the sheep for they know that at end it is all that matters. It is not seminary or any kind of educational accomplishment; it is not the contacts or the connections, the denominations or the devotions to a man, but God's grace and His name glorified. The *called* are people of faith and true believers in the essence of the word believe. They rely, trust, and depend on GOD. They indeed are men and women in the faith and walk; they are *called*.

Hold on to the One who *called* you

Chapter 3

Bearing of Witness

The bearing of witness of the *called* is highly essential as affirmation of God's calling. The bearing of witness is when other anointed men or women confirm God's *calling* on your life. Throughout biblical history this antecedent is revealed. And in our time, to think that men and women should run through the seminary hallways and out the other door with a degree and that qualifies them for the work of the ministry, is reckless and devoid of Godly spirituality. If there is a time when Bearing of Witness is more important it is in our time. We are in a confused time in history and the church is challenged as the transformer of the world we live in.

In my introduction I briefly mentioned the words of confirmation spoken into my life by the prophecy of Silas and others that will be forever vivid. These are Silas exact words, "no matter what you do you are *called* to do the work of the LORD." Never really thinking much of its significance, I moved on with my existence living by my plan, but the older I grew the more fervently these particular words hunted me.

Years went by and the yearning to serve the Lord continued to pull me towards the things of God. At the same time, my desire to fulfill the flesh and all the entrapping of worldly success was to me reality. I saw myself even at this point in my life with a series of dreams and visions, but I never related them to God drawing me ever closer to Him until 1985. In the later part of 1985 I was giving a clear prophetic warning to a certain group of friends about an impending trip they had been planning to take the following day. And, as a matter of fact I was to be part of this trip but the spirit made it quiet clear that "they were not to proceed or else each of the four would be arrested and confined." Their response was that of mockery, 'who made you a prophet' I was asked by one them. They continued with their plan of travel only to find themselves entangled with the law and summarily deported. Today I have lost verbal communication with each but I know where they are. I am sure that none has forgotten to respect the prophetic word of God.

Prior to this year in particular, the enormous attraction of the work of the apostles and Jesus rested in my heart in every way. In 1979/80 I decided that I was going to visit those places I read about in the bible portraying the life of Apostle Paul and his journey of evangelism. I traveled to Greece to fulfill the longing deep down in me in search of history and the ministry. I ended up living in Greece for the next six years before moving to the United States. As time passed, a greater desire to serve the Lord became apparent to me but for some strange reason the so-called American dream of earthly accomplishment kept pressing, which led me to delve into various kinds of business. I experienced some earthly success and as well some failures, or might I say life lessons.

I was given a prophecy by evangelist Lizzy that I would travel through the airports of the world to evangelize for the glory of the Almighty God. Living in Greece I recall a prophecy in a trolley by a complete stranger telling me of what a man of God I would be.

While on one of my trips prophet Glory prayed for me but before the prayer commenced he looked directly at me, shook his head and smiled for a moment. I wondered why. We began the prayer and as we finished he fell back into his seat, he straightened forth both of his palms open and said this to me, "brother, you have been running for too long. Let me say to you that success you will have whether in U.S.A. or Russia nevertheless, God is asking me to tell you tonight that until you come to serve the Lord everything you have including your current wife, will fly through your hands." This came to pass almost two years later. I had achieved becoming a homeowner, being married, and having a second child. I was also an international businessperson who shipped cargos overseas and then everything came crashing down with my wife walking out of the marriage.

The office of an apostle "first witness" for me came from a woman who was instrumental in the starting of The Bible Church of His Will, known as evangelist Peggy. It was in 2002 that I had sent some documents of the church to her and as I was about to leave we stood on the street corner still talking on the issue concerning the church formation, when Peggy said these words, "pastor can I say something to you, do you know that that there is apostolic anointing on your life?" I was immediately enamored at the notion. Peggy with her amiable and beautiful smile looked at me and said, "You will find out soon." And she was certainly right with that spoken word on that day. I thank God for her days of service to the church, to me, and I am eternally grateful to her.

Years later, Apostle Al confirmed the same prophecy given by Lizzy, as he told me, "You are called as a pastor's pastor." In his words, "apostle I see you traveling across the globe teaching pastors how to become good shepherds of God." I have seen myself speaking to crowds of thousands of people, sometimes in an open stadium with people stampeding against themselves to hear and see God's work being done through me.

In 2004, again evangelist Lizzy looked at me after one of our prayers and said these words, "oga sir!" (As they would say in Nigeria as sign of respect) she said, "You really do not know who you are in the Lord, but you know that you are *called*, but I am telling you that God has *called* you as an apostle." And so the weight of who I was to become began to set in at that moment, yet I was trembling and it remains even now as I write. Saints of God there must be the bearing of witness and personal encounter with God, for the one *called*.

Through the account of history in the bible we read about the witness of Jesus' by John the Baptist in the gospels Matt. 3:16, Mark

3:9-11, Luke 3:4, and John 1:6. We can not stop here for the same is said of God and his encounter with those that He called. Such examples are with Noah in Genesis 6:13-end, with Abraham in Genesis 12, with Moses at the Burning Bush in Exodus 3:4-6.

Some might say, well, I just felt that the church was the place for me. That is good if you find yourself to be one in position. The church of God ought to be the place for anyone, and as a matter of fact you are part of the church. We thank God for you that you have found Him, but in this context the witnessing must be obtained for the one *called*. Also, I know that some will debate that going to the seminary before discovering one's *calling,* is the order of things, and there is nothing wrong with it. My argument here is that it is not where you are going or where one will choose to go that dictates or necessarily precedes the *calling*. Those with some kind of denomination group may as well posit that their organization is led by anointed men and women who chose to be in the position they may have found themselves in, and in that thinking they see nothing wrong with how they came to their calling.

All these circumstances do happen but the attesting always comes through long before most of these scenarios, and often they come through strangers and individual personal encounters with God. I am also aware that not all experiences are like those I have listed above or yours truly, but the fact remains that there is witness to every assignment long before the manifestation and therefore the bearing of witness is indispensable.

We in this time must not resolve to mediocrity but we must look back to the ways God has worked and allow God to lead us. The church will be better served if those in the gathering and in the seminaries will be awoken to this consciousness of truth, that the bearing of witness is important and is the answer to effectual church leadership.

Be blessed understand that His assignment must be witnessed.

Chapter 4

My Midfield Avenue Visit; My calling

With all the many witnesses and confirmations received yet my *calling* was that of a personal encounter with the LORD. I was on 7706 Midfield Avenue, in the Westchester area in Los Angeles, in a home I would lose before my full journey with God fully began. The prophecy given to me by prophet Glory of losing all was now taking place; my wife was gone and my business adventure collapsed. With $65,000.00 of equity in my home every effort to sell it for nine months was fruitless. The home listed with three different known agencies in the Los Angeles area and with a reduced price in 97/98 when the market was the envy in the real estate business. Every shed on the market sold for twice or three times its value, yet mine was not to be bought.

Looking back, God had blinded the eyes of all because my deep intention was wrong-headed. I was to continue my business if the equity in the house was realized but the LORD was not having it. I lost my home and for a moment was homeless, and this became the defining moment of truth that God was to have it no other way than for me to fulfill this *calling* to serve. Every negative thought gripped me. I saw nothing but hopelessness, because I had been stripped. On the other hand and looking back now, I saw how empty I had been and I believe God had known that to be the case. It was at this time coming to terms of the bare shell I was, that I came to my knees, mourning, whaling, and crying out to God.

I received a visitation as I lay prostrate in my bed. An angel of God about 9 ft tall, dark-skinned, walked in as I was soaked wet in my own tears on my bed. Facing the wall on my right side, I tried turning to see the face but I could not. Two different times I made an effort to turn, I could not; for there was a force holding me down. This figure whose face I was not allowed to see, tapped me on my left side to tell me with an audible voice, "God has called you, everything will be alright." Immediately the figure disappeared as I experienced heavy cold and fog that filled the room with clouds. I finally was able to turn after the figure left the room.

Upon turning the opposite direction the figure came back and at this time, again I could not see the face. Then came the same exact tapping and exact words "that all will be alright" and the figure disappeared as the chill and cloudiness filled the room with me being overcome at this time with cold. It was only at this point was I able to rise and then became aware of what had happened. I had experienced God as you can read in the bible where Moses saw God face-to-face. Yet no one has seen His face except His glory and the presence of His glory. And from that moment I was not to be the same.

My spiritual journey began full-speed from here on out with more visions, prophesies, healing, casting and laying of hands on people both in the spirit and natural. My prayer life as well changed from simple prayer to a high priestly manner of prayer. In the late nineties I had an experience that I did not understand at the time, of God causing me to eat His Word. I experienced in the spirit a struggle that demanded of me chewing and swallowing a book of which I refused. The person or figure of a man repeatedly requested, yet I insisted not to. And then this figure of a man whom I now realize was an angel, sat on me and forced the book into my mouth with his giant hand over my mouth and said, "You must eat and swallow my Word." This hand made sure every bit of the Word was swallowed before I woke up.

Even before I thoroughly knew what and whom I had been *called* to be, men and women of faith called me by various titles, like Moses or ambassador. I shied away because it never mattered much to me, until *God* confirmed it to me. For me this came in a vision. I was set aside *in the spirit* with a name across my chest in a priestly robe. In a High Ordination celebration great praise and worship was taking place and there was a mighty crowd. There were seven of us apostles all lined up. I had my daughter who wanted to sit and I asked one of the attendants whether it was alright for her to be seated on one of the seven chairs lined up for us. The answer given was "No, for the chairs are for the apostles." My daughter was taken from me to where her fellow children were seated, and the vision ended with the chief priest laying hands on the apostles.

About three years later (before my father's departure into heavenly glory) I saw my father in a vision being asked who he thought I was. Twice he was silent and the third time he said "he is my son Uche," and the voice of the Angel of the LORD said to him, "he is not Uche, he is my apostle, and you are to call him Apostle Uche." My father then called me Apostle Uche and then I arose from the vision.

The next vision of my apostolic office confirmation was that of an angel and I gathered for prayer and healing and at the end he stood out and asked "who will lead us in prayer?" Before anyone was to answer he called me out with these words, "you are the apostle amongst us, and you lead us." Standing as I offered the prayers in closing, he said this to me, "many have walked away from you; you are to receive them when they come back apostle." I was called forward and he said, "Read 2 Cor. 2:8." It was exactly at 3:00 am as I stood and opened my bible and was overcome by the awesome glory of God's revealed truth as I read in the bible a confirmation of what the angel had just spoken, and I have sworn to uphold it.

I have continued to be *called* out in the Spirit as an apostle to lead in prayers and to lay hands on those that are sick. After all this, I was in awe yet afraid to bear this title for well over a year. It is with humility and fear that I walk knowing the overwhelming responsibility I have been given. Positions of influence and power have been foretold in my life with leaders and governments of the world and so, let those who will choose to read this book at any point in time be reminded that when the blabbing mouths says, "that is not of God," or the whispers of naysayers peddle their lies, know that the calling of God is *God's Calling* and that steadfast servants of God are always inheritors of His promises by His grace in resolve.

As the confirmation of God and others came I grew more comfortable and also with the encouragement of my beloved wife, Deborah. I presently have carried the title of an apostle with humility for more than eight years now. Not only was I intimidated but I was gripped with fear by the enormity of this servant position. I look forward to God to enlarge my spiritual territory in His appointed time. Some in certain quarters think that as an apostle I should by this time be a success and to them I say, thank you for your thoughts in all good conscience, but know that it is all in God's timing.

These are the few testimonies of my *calling* and others' confirmations of whom God used to bring richness into my life. Like Apostle Paul and the account of his Damascus road experience with Jesus, these are the recitations of events for me with Jesus. God has *called* me out for His glory and my *calling* from God is uniquely designed for me. It is clear that part of Paul's strength was his clear assignment from the Damascus experience. It is true that all are not going to have similar experiences, but Paul's call was unique. Many in his time struggled and doubted him, and so in my own circumstance I understand that to be accepted by all is unlikely.

Assignments of God's *calling* can never please all. We therefore must resolve whether our agenda is of God or self. Is our righteousness of God or self-righteousness? Paul's mind was made up not to do man's will but God's will. Not to be a pleaser of people, but Christ preached. Paul's assignment which came from Jesus Christ on the road to Damascus would lead to his determined conviction and persistency. Like Paul, I am determined to do the same in persistency and the convictions of my experiences knowing whose I am in this journey in the Lord. It is this clear assignment which has caused the fire of conviction in me to burn so unquenchably. And also the infectious love that I have for Him that exudes whether in my preaching, teaching, or dancing for the Lord. Those that have had the opportunity to see me dance know that it is only part of my expression of what I feel about God, because that will never be enough to express what I know of Him. I am privileged with a special relationship with my God.

So many theologians have written much about Paul with their own spin of what they thought may have been racing through Paul's mind during the time of his writing. One thing that we must never fail to forget about Apostle Paul is that his Damascus spiritual experience determined his conviction and dictated his writings. My writings in this book may well be a challenge to some, but please remember that I have been touched by the hand of the Most High and so I write the truth with fervor for the one who has *called* me.

My dear brothers and sisters in Christ, the work of the LORD is not easy. It can be very challenging and lonely and I am a living witness. Over the years I have had to deal with certain people and their attitudes about the things of God. Some of these behaviors and attitudes have bordered on pure ignorance, others on jealousy and pride (the root of all evil). Incidentally most of these characters are within the body of Christ. I say the body because they claim to be Christians, or academic professors of the things that are about God. What do I mean? It astonishes me how a mere mortal can declare that God no longer calls out apostles. Where, and what bible does any of these men or women of God read from where He informed them of such in the present age? The truth is that such claim has no foundation biblically or spiritually. God is God who does His work with His people, and is still calling out His people for His glory.

Well, with due diligence and respect to diverse thoughts I would answer the wondering mind with an old African axiom, "You can tell the blind that there is no red tomato color in the bowl of soup that is given and he or she agrees because of the blindness, but you cannot tell him or her that there is no salt or pepper in the same soup they are given. Why? Because tasting it he or she can tell." As a man with an apostolic call on his life, I have tasted and continue tasting the bowl of soup and I can tell and agree with the bible account when it states, "A voice came from heaven." I have received similar voices of instructions to deliver in many instances and have been sent out by God's grace with respective messages and healing. They have seen the manifestation of those visions over the years, and experienced the mysteries of the power of God. I understand that some will question and doubt in the absence of any spiritual experience because they see not beyond the natural realm of man.

Some denominational teachings over the years denied the existence of the Holy Spirit, and even went further to propagate that the only apostles were those that walked with Jesus. When confronted with Apostle Paul who never walked with Jesus nor saw Him, they weave there discombobulated explanations. The bible is very clear on the offices and how they are called. The sadness I feel in my heart so frequent is the lack of knowledge of the Word of God by those who proclaim Him.

Those *called* are called by God, not denominations, not individuals. In the Bible we read from the book of 1 Corinthians 12:28, "And God has appointed in the church, first apostles, second prophets, third teachers, then miracles, then gifts of healings, helps, administrations, various kinds of tongues." Ephesians 4: 11-14 states:

And He gave some as apostles, and some as prophets, and some as pastors and teachers, for the equipping of the saints for the work of service, to the building up of the body of Christ; until we all attain to the unity of the faith, and the knowledge of the Son of God, to a mature man to measure of the stature which belongs to the fullness of Christ.

These two texts define the spiritual office of God to all those that debate about the validity of it. Maybe this is not the bible their words are proclaimed from.

And it is for this I frown at churches that call *everyone* a pastor, and we wonder the wounds caused to God's children because man has decided to promote whom God may not have had intentions on elevating.

Short and clear, a pastor is a shepherd to be *called* forth by God. It is not by some kind of academic accredited scholarly attainment, nor paper evidentiary, nor denomination. Another point to be made is in Ephesians 4:13 (this should be a litmus answer to our education that chooses to question the anointing of Lord or want to delimit God), "Have we all attained the unity of faith, and the knowledge of the Son of God? Have we all come to a mature man to the measure of the stature which belongs to the fullness of Christ?" The answer is no, and that is why God is still, *calling* out His people to do His work for His own glory.

Now regarding my position of office of apostle, I would have no objection myself being called a pastor if that is the office I had been given. Rather, that is one of the functions I perform. But to those who have not understood beyond the title of pastor, that is not what God has called me; and to them I would have liked to feel their pain, but I cannot for such is not my burden. The *calling* of God is all that matters and scripture talks about those He has *called*. He has *called* me, and the gifts and the *calling* as we know are irrevocable (Romans 11:29).

Walk in His *calling*!

Chapter 5

The Grace of God; Not a License to Sin

It is neither he that willeth nor desires that brings about a *calling*, but the love of God for His people and His Kingdom and for His glory, nothing more and nothing less. The Grace of God is not a new concept with God and His people. As we glance from the beginning of time privileged through the biblical accounts of history, we see the river beds of grace run throughout the bible from Genesis to Revelation. For some the New Testament is the discovery of grace but for me I posit that grace has been from the beginning of creation. It stems from Adam and Eve, to Noah, and to Abraham, Moses, the prophets, and through the time that Our Lord and Savior Jesus Christ appeared on earth pointing us to who the Father is. It is in the sovereignty of God's grace, which was and still is. We never earned it as a pay check (no work of our hands produced grace), never merited it (no good point or value of ours) here on earth; it was and still is God's love for his own.

The grace of God is like a father who tells his four year old son not to go close to the edge of a cliff but knowing his son is not aware of the consequence of his actions, the father rushes to the bottom and catches him even though he disobeyed. You may say, "Well of course a child that age would not understand." But the analogy here is that God's omniscience is like this father watching over us and clearing danger ahead of us, even while we are breaking His heart by living in sin and rebellion. This is the grace that God extends to us through love that he would save us even before we could give him thanks or understand the great price He paid for us. The father will always love his son because he is bone of his bone, and flesh of his flesh. How much more does grace and the love of God extend to his own creation!

What we must remember is that grace can not be earned by us. In the garden when left on our own, we sinned. When Moses brought the law, we could not keep it, we rebelled. Even after Christ died for us and we heard about it, and witnessed it we still sinned. We deserved to be cut off from a Holy God. But God had mercy on us and provided the perfect sacrifice to atone for our sin and that in itself is the gift of His grace; something we received that we did not, and could not earn.

Reading from the bible in Genesis 1:1-2, "the formless and void earth with darkness received light by His grace." Genesis 6:1-4, Noah's story shows the grace of God; Genesis 11 and 12, Abraham receives grace from God, and in the time of Jesus Christ we read in John 1:17, "For the Law was given through Moses, grace and mercy were realized through Jesus Christ." The implied understanding here is that Jesus Christ brought us the full comprehension of grace which has always been. It is by the grace of God individuals are called out for the work of the Kingdom and it is through the same we are enabled by the Holy Spirit to accomplish His divine will and purpose.

Jesus Christ died for our sin in order to reconcile us with the Father. He brought renewal from a marred state giving us a righteousness that was spotless. It is because of this that we can offer up our worship of God which is the reason for our creation. Through worship and obedience to God our hearts and minds are renewed. Can we say that a Christian who walks in constant disobedience is not saved? No, but their constant life of disobedience represents a home wired with electrical outlets with switches, but no power to bring forth light, rather a scene of darkness. Only when the switches are turned on, does the light shine. It takes the devoted life of obedience for the Spirit of grace which is of truth, the guiding light of the Spirit, the counselor of that truth, Comforter of the truth and the Strengthener who is the Holy Spirit, to enable us to attain maturity and wisdom for fulfilling the purpose of God so that a change can occur. It is the pure grace of God that gave mankind the Holy Spirit while in a fallen state of depravity. Even though He knew humanity in its wickedness would reject Him, God would stoop so low to grant us His merciful grace unto restoration. Man is totally and completely lost without the Holy Spirit To every serious believer in Christ have you found yourself act a fool on the road only to be pricked with a guilty feeling, that is the provision of the Holy Spirit that unctions us to do what is right. It is as a result of the grace of God, His love, and pure favor unmerited.

Other examples of those who by the grace of God were able to do great works for His glory are the prophets; John the Baptist, Jeremiah, Isaiah, Amos, Micah, Elijah, Elisha, and the earlier apostles, the early century church, medieval period, and in our present dispensation. We also see the evidenced work of many others not mentioned but known by their enormous commitment to the assignment to which they were *called* by His grace for the glory of God. The mistake of humanity is the thinking that grace belongs to mankind and can be given out as we see fit.

But the truth is that grace belongs to God and is unmerited, and undeserving on our part. Humanity gives grace on the condition of self-interest and motivation, but with God it is purely based on His love for us. And we know that God is love, 1 John 1: 4: 8. Because this is the essence of God, humanity cannot in anyway give the same grace like Him. Man can copy the behavior or the act of grace and at-will retrieve their gesture of grace. Grace was given to all humanity so that we who are unworthy can now become worthy through Jesus Christ. We can now come to know the Father; it is at this point, as His children, God seeks an acceptable life style of obedience from us.

The grace of God which is based on His love for us, does not exclude us from obedience to His commandments. Noah received commandments from God; he obeyed and was saved. Abraham obeyed God after receiving marching orders to proceed to a foreign land; there he received the visitation of God which made him the father of all nations. Had Abraham disobeyed God his blessings would not have been realized. Moses was chosen by grace to lead his people through the journey in the wilderness, until the children of Israel entered into the Promised Land. God gave commandments on how they were to conduct themselves which they followed, or were disciplined when they disobeyed. And for Moses, we know that he did not enter the promise land either for disobedience or for ungodly temperament, but you the reader can answer on your own.

Jesus Christ obeyed His father by repeatedly declaring He has come not to do His own will, but the will of the father who sent Him. In Gethsemane, according to the Mark account, Jesus Christ offered this prayer in Mark 14:36b, "Yet not what I will, but what your will." So with respect to grace where do we get the absolution of obedience to God? In all narratives of God with His people past and present, there has always been from God requisition for obedience in our relationship with Him and the events of it.

I had in the recent past a visitor in our church with a warped understanding about the grace of God, which means to them that no matter how I live my life and what I do, God understands because He is all about love. I reminded them that while God is of grace He is also the God that requires us to be obedient. God understands the fragility and the futility of humanity and yet He requires from us a certain level of obedience and commitment for His glory. And it is through the saving grace of God we can be perfected in maturity.

None of us can be perfect neither were those who were before us. The biblical characters mentioned in this chapter were all mortal men like the rest of us, but in the assignment given to them God demanded a lifestyle that pleased Him. This lifestyle is obedience, holiness, humility, integrity, honesty, love, and the hunger for righteousness and justice for His people. These people died to self and sacrificed to become the legacy of which God used and is using to tell His story on earth in order that we might know Him. The *called* are called like none other because they have a heart of righteousness. What do I mean? They were bendable to be used.

Children of God, know that some of your professional ministers whom you have been exalting have for too long lied to you because the intentions of their heart to begin with was never right; therefore they teach you garbage. And these are those who teach that Jesus Christ dyeing on the cross is all that you need.

Christ did not die on the cross that you might have the license to sin. It was Jesus that told the Samaritan woman to "go, but sin no more" (John 8:11). He did not condemn her because Jesus did not come to judge the world; He came to show us the road to the Father.

The healing at Bethesda reveals that Jesus found the man in the temple after the man had been healed previously, and Jesus gave him this instruction in John 5:14, "Behold, you have become well; do not sin anymore so that nothing worse happens to you." Jesus Christ never condoned sin contrary to the teaching of some. Jesus Christ knew the weight of sin and its consequences which are deadly. Far be it from the thinking that Jesus Christ at any point was accepting of sin. His chastisement of the Pharisees was about what? It was their sin.

The apostles who walked with Christ, and Paul who came after them who wrote thirteen of the twenty-seven chapters of the New Testament, all preached against sin and taught the true essence of grace. Where do the so called present ministers get their exemptions from? Apostle Paul warns the Thessalonians in 1 Thess. 4:7, "For God did not call us to uncleanness but to holiness." He was a first century man greatly used by God; his time was even closer to the time of Christ.

Let's look at Apostle Peter who walked with Jesus, writing about sin in 1 Peter 1:15-16, "But like the Holy One who called you, be holy yourselves also in all your behavior, because it is written, YOU SHALL BE HOLY, FOR I AM HOLY." Peter references the same commandment given in the Old Testament through Leviticus starting with chapters 11, 18, 19, 20, and 21. Apostle Paul on the issue of grace reminds us that because grace is there for us does not mean we should incubate in sin (paraphrased). He was clear when he stated in Romans 6:1-2, "What shall we say then? Are we to continue in sin so that grace may increase? May it never be! How shall we who died to sin still live in it?"

Paul did not stop there in his definition of the true meaning of grace but went further to explain it in great detail in Romans 6:15-23. Also in Titus Paul lays out what grace is about and what and where true believers ought to be in their walk with Christ. In Titus 2:11-12 he states, "For the grace of God has appeared bringing salvation to all men instructing us to deny ungodliness and worldly desires and live sensibly, righteously, and godly in the present age." There is no question that the mark of a serious believer is to live the life that glorifies God. That life is a life that encompasses the list stated earlier in this chapter. There are so many who lift up Romans 3:9-18 as the ticket of exemption from sin, yet while I agree that we are fallen people which is really Paul's discourse here, Paul spoke passionately against sin.

That grace of God is on the other hand His love for us. But like we on earth expect our earthly children to be obedient in all the requirements we make of them, God our creator and Father requires obedience and holy living from us. The loving God is the one who calls on each and every one of us whenever, and however, with gifts based on His sovereign will. I want to end this chapter with an experience and somewhat of a story.

It had been about three years since finishing my second graduate degree in Theology and Ministry from a well-known Seminary in Southern California, when I had a unique experience which was at the same time tragic. It is one of those life challenging experiences for this particular family. The father and mother were both highly educated people rising in the ranks of academia. I loved them because I could tell they were wonderful people and I knew that they loved God's people. Both had sacrificed for the kingdom and had been blessed to travel to other parts of the world. I share this because our experiences were somewhat shared in the class.

The life altering situation in this family was about one of the professor's children becoming a lesbian; painful to know and accept. The father shared that he accepted his daughter by being reconciled with a Scripture in Romans 11:32, which to me was a total misuse and misapplication of the scripture. Whether directly, or indirectly, he was justifying the situation before us. I could tell that many of my fellow students were disquieted to say the least and some if not many, voiced their objection.

It had troubled me that he was justifying part of the lifestyle with the test of scripture that should not be used as such. But I could see him doing what some parents do when they are confronted between self and God. I remember warning that I have been called by God, and did not just wake up one morning and decide that I would now serve God, nor just come to seminary to enhance my academic profile, as I expressed that grace is not an excuse to sin.

So I decided to do what I do best, which was to anguish and cry out to God for revelation as to the situation. Hear what God gave me as an answer which the very next day I declared about his situation. God said this to me, "My grace can not be measured-out at the expense of who I AM." Now, let the reader pause for a moment and understand what God is saying in this prophetic message… I am God and I am Grace, therefore to excuse sin, or comfort it is to dishonor Me. My friends, grace cannot be used for manipulation so when you hear people use the Word of God for self-justification, if you have been given the grace of the knowledge God's truth, please do not be silent. Defend the Gospel, for God is watching and listening.

Amen.

Chapter 6

Knowing God Intimately and Not Knowing Him

Knowing God and having a relationship with God can be full of Joy and at the same time scary. To know God is to be gripped with reverential fear of His awesomeness. I do not know about others, but I am, and I pray that it is the case for me until my days of eternity.

In the previous chapter I mentioned how I gained the boldness to wear the title of an apostle, after overcoming the ashes of timidity as a result of the enormity that the office exudes. Part of the reason for walking tall with the office is the assurance of knowing that, I know that I know that God has called me at such a time for His glory. God as well has never failed to use me showcasing to His people who He is in me, whether in healing or other supernatural gifting. I have been used to bring forth miraculous healing both in the U. S. A. and Nigeria.

God has even demonstrated His powers through me with a pastor friend in restoring life to a clinically declared dead patient at a hospital in Southern California. That pastor is a living witness. Another pastor as well was healed at a hospital in the same area he lives and can testify himself. Years ago a bishop whose wife has a great gift of prophecy experienced the wonderful gift of God's power through me as he lay dying in the hospital room in Long Beach. Countless others know how the grace of God has used me to touch their lives. I have had prophecies upon prophecies with manifestations.

The 9-11 tragedy I saw the morning before it happened. My sister who resides in Utah is alive to testify as I called her that morning asking her to join me in prayer against such a catastrophe. The shuttle challenger I saw before it happened these are all recorded; the killing of Osama Bin Laden I saw and in my notation I wrote this, "I see Osama Bin Laden caught but life will be lost including his." That was on April 20, 2004. He died on May 2, 2011.

To a pastor friend and another who is an attorney, I expressed that Obama will win re-election. Prior to his re-election, there was a terrorist attack on the United States embassy in Benghazi. I had foretold on the attack that was to be before my church, that Republicans would blame Obama thinking they will use that to scuttle his chances of election, but in the end I saw Obama being re-elected. Funny enough the attorney friend took me out to an exclusive restaurant and asked me to invite a pastor friend who is alive, and they both can testify to this. All prophecies I have documented with dates and a great many of my notations are listed for posterity. To paraphrase my wife, "when the sovereign God has called you why care what humanity thinks."

But despite all these, I have been shocked at the ubiquitous of God's people and their arrogance. A great many of these are sadly in the church and in the seminary with the buffoons who call themselves authors (professors) and finishers of God's work on earth, yet a great many lay in the bed of high arrogance. One particular pastor is a man I love, and for awhile I thought that we both could be used together for a greater work for the glory of God, but I continue to see dimed lights on that end. This brother, a friend in the faith, has a huge problem with my title as an apostle.

Some ask why I should be known as an apostle, that it is not acceptable because people in the United States do not know about apostles. Rather I should be called a pastor like the rest and be comfortable with that. For awhile I could not understand this reasoning until I came to the simplest realization that humanity and their prideful intentions is always in conundrum.

On one occasion I was invited to speak and my name was not even listed on the brochure. When confronted the reply was "I was better in incognito." Over time I had to confront him and admonished him that if God has called me as pastor that I would gladly be known and be proud of it, but not when God has repeatedly warned me and told me this is what and whom "I have *called* you."

My pastor brother told me one day that he was on his way to have surgery and he had been crying out to God for healing. As he headed towards my home he asked God if he could receive his healing through me by God's grace and in his testimony he said this to me, "God said to me, only if you are willing to accept whom I have called him to be, and he said "yes Lord" and God said to him "go then." On that very day he drove down to my place, parked on the street and in his car I laid hands on him and he received healing instantly and never went to the doctor as of the time I am writing.

This brother confessed to me his jealousness of the anointing on my life wondering why he could not be used like I am. Thanking him for his honesty, I comforted him and advised that jealousness is not appropriate rather if we can die to self we all can compliment each others gifts. One of the last recent visits to his evening church services, an Australian gifted in prophecy whom I have never met before, said this to me before his parishioners prophesying he called me, "Sir you are the ambassador of Christ. There is no other office before God greater than yours. He added that I am going through a lot and will yet go through more stuff." The same night and a moment later my friend's wife who is as well gifted, spoke and said, "Uche look at the red carpet that is laid for you. I see you walking along this carpet and there is a huge celebration before you." Now if these people that know me and know all this about me, cannot bring themselves to accept who God has called me, it speaks voluminous to the issues God's people often are encompassed with.

I have had some old acquaintances whose Baptist indoctrination cannot bring them to accept who God has called me to be. They cringe to hear me be introduced as an apostle and these people and their obtuse behavior to me is beyond ignorant. One other known pastor thought I could be a candidate for their denomination but the trade-off was that I would not be allowed to use the title "apostle" even though it is what God called me. I said, are you kidding me, I refuse to deny God to serve humanity and their perfidy. And that was the end of that chapter. Sadly, humanity finds comfort in the conferred earthy titles of man or woman rather than that which God has spoken; what a shame.

Funny thing recently happened on a Sunday morning on our way to church. My wife had stopped to get her Starbucks coffee. She ran into an old acquaintance who was a youth pastor at a former church. He was younger compared to me, and they spoke for a moment. My wife proceeded to introduce me to him saying, "This is my husband Apostle Uche Nyeche." The pastor turns around to me and declares, "Okay, I will call you Pastor Uche." He determined what he wanted to call me, not what I was introduced as; what a temerity. Can we see governors and call them mayors, generals and call them majors, representatives and call them senators?

My office is one chosen by God. Saints of God cannot be right when 'to give honor to those who honor is due' is a problem, especially in the church and especially by those who claim to be pastors. The Word is clear and such is the instruction in Romans 13. It begs the question whether not knowing God is the reason for the difficulty, or the desire to worship rational humanity instead of God. To choose not to obey God and His word is to not serve Him regardless of one's claim. The reader should note that in every negative experience one encounters in this life, and trust that one will fall on your lap at some point in life's journey, there is always an exception.

I met a wonderful pastor in the second location that we met as a church. This man understood the purpose for which he is a pastor. He knew it was not about him but God, and that glory and honor belonged to our God. After months of meeting and asking if we could gather in his building, he prayed about it and consulted his board. The day I met him for the final answer he threw the keys to the building and said to me, "I believe you are *called* to do the work of God, you can use this place without a charge." We worshiped there five years and he literally refused us paying a dime.

It does not matter whether one is *called* pastor or a seminary professor, there are many who have been in church for 20-30 years and still they are tormented with issues of pride, arrogance, jealousy, greed, and hate. These people can deny all they want the deep conflicts they have but these are major issues that are contrary to the ways of God. I have a great reverence for God and so the instinctive thought for me is that to honor God is to honor His chosen and when you dishonor His chosen, you dishonor God. At least that is what I know of the word of God. In addition, the scriptures in 1 Chronicles 16 and Psalm 105 say, "Touch not my anointed and do my prophets no harm." Simply put, that anyone who has a problem in honoring those whom God has *called* to speak the truth and stand against sin, does not yet thoroughly know God because knowing Him is to be umbrage with some of what I have thus far mentioned.

These nameless pastors are not bad people at all. I think for the most part they mean no harm. Some of them have blessed me tremendously and I remain thankful to God for them and their ministry. I continue to pray for them, their families, and that God in His benevolent grace will bless them to walk with integrity and boldness in their calling.

Now I leave these thoughts with the reader. You may have been confronted with some of the things I have mentioned here. You may have been rejected by others in your circle, told that you are imagining things, or hallucinating…common phrases of those spiritually ignorant. You may have even compromised in order that you may be accepted and belong, or allowed your denomination to give a title befitting of man and not what you know God has *called* you. Here you read about my *calling*, the confirmations by others, evidence of God using me to prove His hand on my life. You have thus far read about my uncompromising stand in knowing Him and honoring Him and you must understand by now that my desire is to please God and to impart to you a deeper understanding of who He is.

When we search out the existence of Christ in Christianity it never fails that there is ample evidence not only of his existence but there is written, physical, social and economical evidence of his existence just to name a few. There are original manuscripts of the Holy Bible that have been preserved for all to view. There are also graves discovered bearing the names of people in the bible and non-biblical sources that confirm the identity of Jesus along with many others.

This information helps us intellectually to identify with something true. If we are convinced that something or someone is true, we are then at liberty to trust. In reading the story of God and His Son Jesus' love for us, I cannot recount the many times that the Holy Spirit has made himself real to me. You see, since I know that Jesus is the son of God and that he died on our behalf raised in Glory, I have a deep love that cannot compare to the love of this world. Jesus desires to know each one of us intimately. God has left us his word that we may know Him and learn to live our lives in victory over sin.

In the beginning of this chapter I described the joy of knowing God, my reverential fear for God, and how fearful it is to be before God. One thing I have yet to mention is the sacrificial cost in standing up against the world's established ways of doing things. In most cases you will find that you are standing alone with no one holding you up except the hand of the living God. What better hand to hold you up than that of Jesus.

My brothers, my sisters in Christ, if you have made the commitment to serve God in truth then be resolute in your steadfastness to honor Him and Him alone, for at the end victory will be yours. I leave you with one of the promises Jesus left us in John 16:33, "Tribulations you will have but be confident that I have overcome." And truly, I have the victory through Jesus because I am His.

Chapter 7

Dangers of Denominations

If there is an ever-present danger to the Church of God today it is in part denominations. Looking back into history of the early church foundation this was not the case. These people genuinely cared about doing God's will and the majority of whom were Africans, helped in molding the present Christian thinking. Some of these theologians were people like Tertullian, Victor of Vita, Augustine, Philo, Cyprian, Synesius, Optatus, Shenut of Atripe, and Verecundus to mention but a few. They were men who varied in their nuance but were God centered. It was not about money for them nor was it much about their denominational doctrines. They were purely faithful people who feared God and were led by God. To be part of them was to know you were serious and called of God. However, after the medieval reformation and those seeking religious freedom landed on the shores of America, the exultation of denominations became the trend.

Denominations are ever-blooming because of humanity's mendacious craft. Unfortunately in all regions of the world including the country of my birth, Nigeria, such is the case. I'll tell you a story. Recently a good friend whom the Lord has blessed me to counsel for years now, called me up to ask my opinion about his intent in joining a predominantly known denomination from Nigeria. Hear his story what this so-called group asked him to do…to seek out three professionals as congregants, and with his degree from the seminary and ten thousand dollar seed money from the denomination for him to start, he then would become a pastor.

My answer to him came in this form, I said to him, "the easy answer you would like to hear from me will be to go ahead and join, but I will preface my answer for you in this manner, pray and allow God to reveal what He has *called* you for." My caution to him was to be careful that money is not the attraction. I also cautioned him to know for sure if God told him that he was to become a pastor in the circle of this denomination.

Now let's think for a moment of this approach. Does this denomination assign and promote despite any knowledge of whether this young man is *called* to be a pastor; he well may have been *called* as teacher. Incidentally teaching is the passion of this young man in talking to him over the years. That a pastor can teach does not mean that a teacher can be a pastor. Hear me God's people, a pastor is a shepherd *called* by God. This attempt by this denomination is one of the reasons why many are misguided and wounded in the churches.

The other reprehensible demand was for this young reverend to recruit three professionals. The aim for that is what? On the surface it may appear to be about membership but at the core is it about money? These professionals will be able to sustain the venture in finances not only for the local church, were there to be one, but also the denominational headquarters. My prayer is that those in leadership of these denominational corporations would raise their moral compass. Are they asking questions about the life style of these professionals? Would it matter if they are swindlers, armed robbers, or child abusers, etc.? The main goal should never be about profit and growth at the expense of integrity.

A great number of pastors are wonderful people but they disregard God's voice to follow their denomination's policy, including their teachings even if it contradicts the very doctrine of our faith.

Today in the United States where many denominations exclude God, they are the ones calling forth people and installing them as pastors whether such individuals are *called* or not. I am not saying that there are no rules or requirements of process, but since when have denominations become the determinant caller of individuals to do the work of God which is not theirs but God's? We wonder why there are hardly any manifestations of healing in churches, because the church has quenched the spiritual anointing from God.

Some churches are busy referring people to psychologists and psychiatrist in cases where the needs are spiritual. I heard from someone that a psychiatrist said, "How they wish the church would do its job, because most of the people referred to him are dealing with spiritual issues." This should be embarrassing to the church. I am not in any way ruling out the work that these professionals do but is the church missing something here? The church is neglecting its responsibility to address spiritual healing. The church must be a place where the Spirit of God reigns and the truth is spoken and not just 'feel good' spoken words. The church should not be mainly a place for social gathering, and sadly in our present time that is what we see in some churches.

Seminaries today have also been impacted by denominational dictates. They have so many students who do not attend church but since they are sponsored through denominations, many are guaranteed to be placed in a church and at times given money to start the church. This is done without reliance on faith in God. Where is the sacrifice we are *called* to endure as we depend on God and learn what faith walk is? Where is the act of learning how to bow before God listening to and hearing His voice directing and leading us for His glory? We wonder why the church is weak, because the denominations have turned the house of God into a business empire. The pastors they assign dare not deviate from their leadership or policy order. This prevents the free movement of the Holy Spirit and will unlikely produce spiritual growth or the maturity needed for true transformation. Denominations become stale when they forget that God is not bound by their interpretation of His Word. Change it all you want, His Word rises from deepest valley to the highest mountain top and will never be contained by man. In some denominations, if the branch is not generating enough funds, the pastor risks loosing his position.

There is a pastor I know in one of the denominations who is always terrified of being replaced because of his church not growing fast enough or generating enough funds to the satisfaction of his corporate headquarters. His fear is not about the spiritual order of the house, but him satisfying those high in the position that can determine whether he remains as a pastor. What a pressure for anyone to be inundated with.

The defense of denominations from those who are a part of the organization is that of financial backing and accountability. Having written on the financial incentives of these groups, the later is an interesting topic that holds a shallow view. I will be bold to declare that no one needs leadership direction that puts man's design above that of God. One can seek guidance but that guidance should not be of a corporate structured model which has not been sifted through the Word of God, and His direction. Who better to lead and direct than God.

I take assault at the thought that any one's ability in obedience to God must be shepherded by a corporate structure. Simply put that if you know God and have reverence for God because you love Him, any act or sanctimonious behavior or overt sin that breaks the heart of God, will be avoided and shunned. To argue that denominations are the warder against ungodly behavior is hyperbole. Many corrupt denominational pastors, bishops, are protected and covered-up for in these denominations. I mince no words; hear this, that some of these criminals with their heinous behaviors ought not to be found anywhere near where God's people gather for church. Denominations may be keeping these predators because of the money generated into their covers. What impact has this had on the body of Christ?

I must state that a few have been removed from their positions yet a great number of others have remained even when their behavior has been questionable. The danger to the body is evident when we view the overall condition of our society. Some of the nonsense we have settled for in these denominations is that the present age is seeking mendacity instead of truth. They are seeking expediency instead of the truth. I have had some friends whose denominations have given them an annulment from a previous marriage to fit the man-made rules not of God because God knows that there was a previous marriage. It is upon this that I do write not to sanction divorce but to render my thought on the "Issue of Divorce," Genesis reminds us that in the beginning God's intention for man and woman was to be joined together as one. He warns, "Therefore let no man (humanity) put asunder the marriage." Marriage for God has and remains a covenant.

I would like to make a point that God continues to see divorce as challenge against his holy law, just as he saw polygamous relationships which were against his law. God used the people of the ancient even when they had experienced divorce, and He also uses divorced men and women for His glory just as well in our present time. This sacred institution called marriage, from Adam the first man God used for His Glory, was intended to be between man and woman. However, the ancient culture of humanity chose to live a polygamous lifestyle. God saw it all, knowing that it was in violation of His Original Covenant of the institution of Marriage in the garden. God looked beyond the fault of humanity and chose to allow His work to be fulfilled for His Glory through those among them He chose.

Jesus in His encounter with the Pharisees in Matthew 19 reminded them that Moses' permission of divorce was because of the *hardness of the heart of man.* Furthermore, this hardness was as a result of the fall of man. The perfect intention of God for humanity was made "imperfect." God's Grace and Mercy will override the fallen state of humanity. Does God hate divorce? The answer is yes. But the end of all sin should point back to the Cross where Jesus has redeemed each and every one of us. Others receive the same annulment so that they can become pastors, because to be divorced makes one morally outcast and heavenly disqualified in their book.

Some have decided that to be *called* is to be married, but they forget that Jesus, who is our model, was never married. I must make this point clear by stating that I in no way fault any one who sought these rights to be made available to them by their various denominations. I must also be clear that this is not in any way intended to make anyone find themselves in the hall of shame. All that I am stating here is the fact that denominations and their rules of exception have no bearing at all to the orders and laws of God. They are nothing but mere manmade rules of earthly comfort which at the end are unpleasing to God whom we claim to proclaim.

Years gone by, I have met those who came from one denomination or the other who have been led to believe that they are unworthy to partake in the Eucharist, communion, also known as the Lord's Supper. I will never forget an experience of a young lady who visited our church and left feeling that she committed an unpardonable sin because she took the Lord's Supper. Over the years I have been blessed to help others come to know that the Lord's Supper is about Jesus. He is the church and as a community in Christ Jesus denying any the participation is to deny them the participation in Him. In the next chapter I will write more on the Lord's Supper in Christian Community/Ministry.

With this said, I must hereby address the independent churches. I am not in any way proposing that the independent churches are the answer. This is farther from the truth, they are just as culpable. There are despicable acts in some these churches as well and because they are small and under the radar, some get away with unfathomable acts. What is the solution? The solution is for the trusting faithful believers to know that there is no evil deed before God that goes unpunished. They should when unsure, test the spirit as they are commanded and if the teaching is contrary to the bible, they should pack-up their bags and seek for a gathering that honors God in truth and is directed by His Spirit. To sit in the congregation of the ungodly is to adjourn ones personal growth with God and their calling.

I am sure that God continues to laugh at the games. I have

often said that God is so much of a good God, so sovereign in His omnipotence, that He allows us to reign in our deceit. The bible has not failed in warning us that any foundation not of God, will crumble often through public humiliation and disgrace, this often exposes the lacking ways of man. Denominations have thrived over the years and continue to. Some professional ministers have and own huge followings. But God shakes His head for He knows His own. If the body of Christ is to rise and flourish we must move from these man-made denominations to a foundation rooted in scripture and directed by proven men of God.

Let us be mindful that without Him leading us, we are doom

Chapter 8

Eucharist or the Lord's Supper in Christian Community/Ministry

My experiences with saints of God who have been misled to focus on their unworthiness in the taking of the Eucharist, Communion, or sometimes referred to as the Lord's Supper, is the reason for this chapter. My desire here is to inform the reader that it is wrong for the church to tell anyone that they are unworthy to take the Lord's Supper but it is up to the individual to decide if they want to partake in the sharing of the body of Christ and drinking of the cup of the new covenant (his blood). The writing then in this chapter is about Joe (fictional congregant) and his problem; a character in struggle and the answer to the question why he should not be denied the Lord's Supper.

We find ourselves confronted with a situation regarding our beloved brother Joe and his struggles with alcohol. I present that Joe should be allowed to partake in the Lord's Supper based on the forgiving life of our Lord and Savior Jesus Christ, the remembrance of him dying on the cross for the sinner, and not for the righteous. I seize this opportunity to lay out briefly my belief in the theological significance of the Lord's Supper, and nature of the Lord's Supper.

For God through his Son has given us a new covenant in His body and blood. It states in John 6:51, "I am the living bread that came down from heaven, whoever eats of this bread will live forever; and the bread that I will give for the life of the world is my flesh." Joe is in need of this life. Whenever we gather, we partake in representation of the risen savior. We must see the presence of Christ even in His absence, as at work in our lives. The effects to the Christians according to J.N.D.Kelly, "The general belief may be summed up by saying that anyone who partook by faith was held to be united and assimilated to Christ, and so to God."[1] The moment of the Last Supper should be viewed as the moment for forgiveness, restoration, renewing of minds and hearts in Jesus Christ.

The Lord's Supper was an institution of gathering that Jesus Christ performed the night before he was crucified. The central purpose of the Lord's Supper is to remember the triumphant work of the cross. It was work that brought us deliverance; to most it is a remembrance of Christ' suffering on the cross. To others it is a solemn time to examine themselves before God. Why? It is an expression of Lord's Supper that reflects the substance union between humanity and the essential nature of God in Christ.

Ray S. Anderson states, "Christ as the objective union of human and divine in his own person is also the objective **Presence** of God to humans and humans to God. All forms and theories with regard to his 'presence' are relative to this objective 'presence' of God in Christ. Again, we must say that the mysterion is located in the incarnate one, not in the mechanical or supernatural relation between physical element and spiritual grace."[2] This is 'the Last Supper' that Jesus shared with his disciples. We read in 1 Corinthians 11:23-25, Jesus took the bread and when he had given thanks he broke it, and said to those with him, "this is my body which is broken for you, do this to call to remembrance."

Jesus also took wine as was of the Jewish tradition, in a cup or chalice and gave to those that were present with him that night and

---

1   J.N.D. Kelly, *Early Christian Doctrine*, (New York, NY: Harper Collins, 1978), 450

2   Ray S. Anderson, Lecture ST516 Theology of Christian Community

he said, "This cup is the new covenant in my blood; do this, as often as you drink it, in remembrance of me" (1 Cor. 11:25). This was known as a Passover meal celebration in commemoration of the Jewish exodus out of Egypt, and it is the Jewish redemption from bondage. The significance of this to Christian's and its meaning is that Christ's victory over death has set us free from bondage of sin, to life in Jesus Christ.

The Eucharist is one of the many names for one of the most important Christian sacraments. The Eucharist is the name still used by Catholics, Eastern Orthodox, the Oriental Orthodox, Anglicans,' United Methodist, and Lutherans. Most Protestants prefer the Holy Communion, the Lords Supper, or Breaking Bread.

In the early church this began with a blessing over the bread and wine associated with a common meal that followed the form of earlier Jewish blessings. Different denominations have shown it to evolve into a broad variety of liturgies. The Roman Church saw the bread and wine to be the actual flesh and blood of Jesus, or transubstantiation as it is called.

"The Eucharist is the communication of the body and blood of the Lord, which as St. Paul testifies, ought to be taken to the end that we might more amply abide and live in Christ, and that he might live and abide more amply in us."[3] For this reason, our partaking together of this Holy Supper in celebration is in order that we might be more and more in Christ for reunification to eat the flesh and to drink His blood. Because this is the reason, it will be essential to establish and manage the order of the celebration so that people are made aware of the need for their participation often in the flesh and blood, and be aware of the profits we get from this message and eating.

The Scriptural reference in 1 Cor. 11:27 "partaking in an unworthy manner" becomes wrong in the interpretation, for Paul was addressing the greed of the rich who having so much, yet was not allowing the needy to partake in an orderly fashion. Therefore

---

3   Benjamin W. Farley, *Colloquium on Calvin Studies*, (Davidson, NC, 1984) 119

using it as the basis to deny Joe to partake denies the meaning of what our Lord Jesus stood for will not be proper. Joe is a believer in Jesus Christ therefore our Lord's redeeming quality is greater than Joe's drunkenness. We should note that Joe's remorse, or shame, is awareness that he is repentant and in itself therefore demonstrates that he is receptive to knowing that God still loves him and there is still a chance for his atonement.

As Ray S. Anderson writes, "Rather, Jesus is the sacrament of saving and sustaining grace that flows through the "sacrament" acts of Baptism and the Lord's Supper, as especially constituted for the Church itself as the sacrament of forgiveness and healing."[4] If we believe that there is forgiveness and healing in the name of Jesus therefore, a broken and repentant heart must be allowed to approach the table.

In his lecture, Ray S. Anderson states, "forgiveness of sin has to do with removing the consequences of sin which, according to Paul, is death."[5] If as Romans 6:23 states, "The wages of sin is death" then rejection of one with the issue of drunkenness may not be the answer but forgiveness, as Jesus so often demonstrated in sacramental grace.

We can also point to the Sacrament of Jesus through His healing of the man with a withered hand in John 12:10-13, "A man was with a withered hand, and they asked him, "is it lawful to cure on the Sabbath?" Jesus showed that the life of a person was more important through his healing of the man, than the law of the Sabbath. In this case, acceptance of Joe, not the alcohol, through the love of the pastor urging him in partaking of the Lord's Supper becomes more of a theological significance than the slighted interpretation of some that one must be righteous in order to partake.

Because the last Supper is Jesus, and Church represents Jesus Christ as the revelation to the world, the very love of God ought to

---

4   Ray Anderson, *The Soul of Ministry* (Louisville, Ky: Westminster John Knox Press) 168

5   Anderson, 168

be in existence amongst the human community of believers. Ray S. Anderson states it clearly, "the human community that comprises the body of Christ is the people of God through whom Christ continues to be present, despite their failure' sinfulness, and disobedience."[6] Joe's failure, being drunkenness, further described as a sin, cannot stop the work of Jesus. Rather the Church ought to demonstrate the sacrament of forgiveness and love thoughtfully.

Looking back to what the bible says about sin, 'that the wages is death' and Ray S. Anderson's argument is that, "one might respond that sin is not a physical disease but a spiritual condition that requires forgiveness, not healing, if someone does wrong to me, it is the relationship that has been ruptured, not my spleen."[7] I can agree in part with Anderson's statement that sin is a spiritual condition but in regards to Joe's condition, and many others, there is a need for forgiveness and physical healing. As part of the human community of Christ, we must recognize the spiritual needs in conjunction with the physical needs in order to allow wholeness in the body of Christ. To all those believers who may have been told that there is something in you or your lives that makes you unworthy, understand that partaking of the Lord's Supper is to join in the celebration so that you can be joined with Jesus Christ.

You are His, be blessed

---

6   Anderson, 170
7   Anderson, 171

Chapter 9

Baptism, Baptized as Infants all you need

Here in this chapter I want to transport the understanding to the many believers who are confused about children or infant baptisms. These are those who feel that it is wrong or even unsure whether it is biblical. I want to let them know that there is nothing biblically wrong in the baptism of any child. I write on this because in our church there was a question about baptizing children. The understanding in this context was that it was alright to dedicate a child but baptism was not accepted for children prior to their spiritual understanding.

The question on this for me was where is this thinking coming out of, because I have yet to teach on the subject? I would have to answer this question myself by concluding that it was nothing but a bad theology put forward which caused this person uneasiness when the issue of this baptism was put forward. The names as you read this chapter is characters who were baptized in their early age yet unsure that their baptism was correct. Please read the dialogue of Dear Bob and Sue, as to why they should be at peace with their childhood baptisms......

As you have requested I will address the meaning of Christian Baptism as it relates to faith for your study so that you may determine whether you want/need to be re-baptized. Bob, as you have shared you were baptized as an infant in the church to which your parents belonged. And Sue, you have shared that you were baptized in a

Baptist church when you were 12 years old, after your confession of faith in Jesus. I hope you will find this information educational as to the history behind baptism and that it will clear the confusion you now feel. At the same time I hope you find this helpful as you study and pray for God's guidance.

After the time of Christ the setting of child baptism was never of controversy in the first and second century church. Those like Pliny, St. Justin Martyr, St. Irenaeus of Lyon, St. Polycarp, and St. Hippolytus all believed in the baptism of children. Controversy or the first opposition that would be recorded was from Tertullian, and his reason was based on false teaching that sin after baptism was unforgiveable. These false teachings led to the reason why many of the early church fathers in the third and the fourth century were baptized late into their adulthood and some of these men were people like St. Augustine, St. Basil, and St. Jerome.

We confront this issue in the Protestant Reformation as Ulrich Zwingli (1484-1531) with his Swedish Reformed Church and his students who sought to be re-baptized. Their reasons for this action were that their infant baptism was invalid because they were not escorted by works of faith. So then can we state that it is un-biblical to baptize infants or children, the answer is NO. Our faith has no bearing to our works; it is given to us through our Lord and Savior Jesus Christ. The bible leaves us with so many examples of infant or children baptism in households at the time of Apostle Paul. Here in this book are the examples for the reader to note....that in 1 Corinthians 1:16, "Now I did baptize also the household of Stephanas; beyond that, I do not know whether I baptized any other." In the book of Acts 16:33b, "immediately he was baptized he and his household." This was the Philippian jailor's household; In Acts 18:8, "Crispus, the leader of the synagogue, believed in the Lord with all his household, and many of the Corinthians when they heard were believing and being baptized." This was the household of Crispus. Also in Acts 16:15, "And when she and her household had been baptized, she urged us, saying, "If you have judged me faithful to the Lord, come into my house and stay." There are other examples mentioned in the bible. These were some households we can assume that there were infants and children which were baptized.

Sue and Bob, with the examples I have given you, your baptism as infants or children are valid and in order. I know there are some groups or denominations that oppose this idea even in our present time but it does not mean they are right in their opposition. When we are baptized as infant we are baptized into the heavenly family. To state that our mind must understand before we believe is to reduce faith to that of human reason, which says it must make sense in order for us to believe. Baptism is performed by our obedience to God and is a voluntarily act.

We are commanded to join with God in the relationship through the covenant He established for us by His Son. One can make the argument that our faith with God is personal and this is indeed true, but that personal relationship is one person with God in their individual journey and does not and cannot be restricted to the lone relationship. Our relationship with God is the totality of the communion of the whole church as a body or group this is the church family. As His children we are part of this family and so to be baptized as a child is to be baptized with Christ. Growing up as a child, I knew that my family was my family; a place that I belonged and my rights were never in doubt. My right could only have been terminated if I chose not to be part of my family.

I have children and they automatically understand that they are part of my family and their right in the family cannot be questioned. I see it with my 14 year old daughter, what belongs to me belongs to her, and nobody can tell her anything different. They can at some point chose to server that bond and that is the only time they are not part of my family. But their remaining in the family is the acceptance of what it entails as rules and their obedience and sacrifice in order to remain. Our family on earth is a replica of our heavenly family. My children who are born into my family identify with the family through their actions same also are we an example of one being born again through baptism into the heavenly family.

J. N.D. Kelly describes baptism as being washed with water and with the Holy Spirit. The person receives the remission of sins. He passes from sin to righteousness. Baptism conveys the positive blessings of sanctification, the putting on of the new man, adoption as God's son by grace, union with Christ.[8] Michael Green states that baptism is something done for you by another, as if to remind you that your salvation is entirely a matter of grace, and not something to which you make any active contribution.[9] This is another reminder that it is by grace. Ray Anderson in his lecture, states Baptism is salvation through faith as a divine act of grace. Is our maturity in the faith any hindrance to the divine work of the Holy Spirit in Baptism? If I apply this thought to you Sue, say that at the time you were baptized you professed Christ; you were in the faith. As you mature in your walk with Christ, you will often look back and see a change. As we look into infant baptism, and whether it is necessary to be re-baptized you may gain more insight as well.

Bob, I know that you are concerned since you were only a child when you were baptized. Here is one perspective that speaks to the view that being baptized once is sufficient without regard to age. Michael Green writes, "If a person has been baptized with water in the name of the trinity, then he must be considered as a child of God, an inheritor of the kingdom of God."[10] In other words, Baptism, like justification, is once for all. It is unrepeatable. It is as Christ's death was once and for all on that cross for our forgiveness.

You will also find the belief that the Holy Spirit dwells, without their knowledge, in baptized infants.[11] In Ephesians 4:5, we read that there is one Lord, one faith, one baptism. Reading in the book Early

---

8   J.N.D. Kelly, *Early Christian Doctrines* (New York, NY: Harper Collins, 1978), 428

9   Michael Green, *I Believe in the Holy Spirit* (Grand Rapids, MI: William B. Eermans Publishing Company, 2004)168-169

10 Michael Green, *I Believe in the Holy Spirit* (Grand Rapids, MI: William B. Eermans Publishing Company, 2004), 159

11 J.N.D. Kelly, *Early Christian Doctrines* (New York, NY: Harper Collins, 1978), 430

Christian Doctrines, it emphasizes that the baptized, even infants, are endowed with the graces of illumination and justification, and are grafted into Christ's body; released from death, they are reconciled to God until eternal life, and from being sons of men receive the status of sons of God.[12] Can the Holy Spirit dwell in a child once they are baptized and yet as one becomes an adult there is a need to join their faith to the experience of baptism? Let us also look a little further.

In 1 Peter 3:21 states, not putting away the body's defilement but the pledge of a good conscience towards God, through the resurrection of Christ. Is it possible to pledge good conscience towards God when you are an infant? Ephesians states that there is one baptism. We also read in Peter that it is a conscious commitment towards God. Knowing that you have already been baptized once but have recently professed your faith in Jesus Christ, I will share a story that may bring peace to the situation.

In Ray Anderson's book, he proposes a situation where a man would not perform marriage because the couple had been divorced, and the bible speaks against divorce. He states that it is not enough to say, "the bible teaches," but they are responsible to recognize that the Word of God was even then incarnate in their midst and acting so as to reveal God's ultimate purpose, which is to liberate persons from the law of sin and death and to free them to recover their humanity as God intended."[13] I believe what we can understand from this that there is liberty in the presence of God. God gave the Word for us to live by but that we must use wisdom in applying it.

In a lecture by Ray S. Anderson, he states, "Faith is not a condition which effectually causes baptism to regenerate, but regeneration through the Holy Spirit effectually binds the human subject through faith to the salvation of Christ.[14] He makes a distinction that faith is indispensable to baptism because the baptism of the Holy Spirit is

---

12 J.N.D. Kelly, 432

13 Ray S. Anderson, The Soul of Ministry (Louisville, Kentucky:Westminster Jon Knox Press, 1997), 8

14 Ray S. Anderson, Lecture ST516 Theology of Christian Community

the effective cause of faith, which allows us to share in the baptism of Christ.

On the contrary, I believe that faith does not have its base in baptism, nor is baptism grounded in faith. Both are based on the fact that God has the power to bring about salvation or redemption through Jesus Christ. In 1Cor 12: 13, Apostle Paul writes that "We were all baptized into one body, unified into one body, and all made to drink of one Spirit." This means that in and through Jesus Christ, we are all complete. It is not the handiwork of man; it is the empowering work of the Spirit in Jesus Christ.

Now to you Bob, as you have shared you were baptized as an infant in the church to which your parents belonged. I hope that the information shared will help to bring understanding to your concern about your faith. Likewise, to you Sue your baptism at age twelve is valid as though baptized as an adult, being baptized then in Jesus Christ. Your Christian assurance of faith does not change. Both of you are baptized unto Jesus Christ by faith.

May you be fulfilled in Him, Amen.

Chapter 10

You the Called

The off-shoot of the roots of your confession should parallel what Apostle Paul said in Philippians 3:8, "Yea doubtless, and I count all things but loss for the excellency of the knowledge of Christ Jesus my Lord: for whom I have suffered the loss of all things, and do count them but dung, that I may win Christ." Not standing up for the one who *called* you is not standing up for anything. It matters less all your Rolex watches and Rolls Royce cars, your private jets, your edifice which we call church and the 'lost' you have, that may be called members. The devil blesses those who bid and win his contract.

Apostle Paul knew who called him and he was willing to sacrifice it all to know Him. This is why I stress the need to be *called* and the knowledge for the reason why you have been *called*. A clear mandate is a confirmed mandate, with conviction like none other. Apostle Paul had such a stanch conviction that when Apostle Peter was about to compromise, Apostle Paul was unafraid to confront him in Galatians 4:11-14. My innate desire for all, as I desire for my self, is that through the grace of the living God we may do the work for which we have been *called* with truth, honesty, integrity, humility (not denying whom we are *called* to be), walking in love for God and dispensing that love for His people. In the previous chapter I mentioned about sacrifice and again, I stress that it is part of the package in following Him. I know that there are some that claim the main theme in the

Bible is the words, bless me. That will be for another topic in another book God willing.

So, to you who have been *called* you must stand up and turn loose from these church groups or denominations. You should now in the name of Jesus Christ our Lord tell the devil to let loose because you are in a false membership that will hamper your growth. If you find it difficult to expunge yourself from them you need to consult the Spirit of the living God to be sure He is the guiding light in your life. For there are two things that are certainly certain it is that light and darkness do not function the same with neutral results. It is either light that produces life, or darkness that steals life. Like Paul, I count all things rubbish in order that I might know Him. God has *called* me and I make no apologies for the sake of man's approval, nor do I seek alliances that will not be for the furtherance of the kingdom of God. I am heart broken to see too many people dancing and running around like ducks for what will not fulfill. Too often I hear from men and women who may be indeed called but hurriedly and effortlessly they are willing to settle for frills. My brothers and sister of the faith, a double minded person is an unstable and untrustworthy person. Such persons even when you are *called* by God you run the risk of your calling fulfillment or be used half of a measure.

Among many of the biblical characters *called* out by God, the *called* of our time in every spectrum must shape their mind and walk firmly with these examples of dedication in doing the work of our God. One of whom I identify so much with in the midst of the other biblical characters, is Prophet Jeremiah who served as a priest known as "the weeping prophet." He was a man torn over the revelations of judgment against his people by the occupying Babylonians. He sought out other nations to obey the warnings of God as well as pleading for the need of his own people to please God. Jeremiah harkened to God's command not to marry nor have children but for him to devote his life to God; and that he did as we read from the biblical account.

Writing this chapter I am reminded of Jeremiah 9: 23-24, Thus says the Lord, "Let not a wise man boast of his wisdom, and let not the mighty man boast of his riches; but let him who boasts boast of this, that he understands and knows me, that I am the Lord who exercises loving-kindness, justice, and righteousness on earth; for I delight in these things, declares the Lord." I have been *called* and in this journey my desire is to please Him. You who are *called* take to heart what it means to forsake things in order that you might know Him. Let your boast be that you have understanding of Him. Apostle Paul reminds us over and over as he declared of himself, to boast in the Lord. You the *called* desisting from the humanity boasting in riches and wisdom and knowing the Lord should be your crisscross by which you are known, as I am also known.

I seek no justification from humanity knowing that their wisdom is foolishness before God. All that matters to me is that I know the Lord and seek His face, including teaching the faithful saints by His grace that He gives me the opportunity to minister to. I have no desire neither do I seek anything that the Lord has not given me, nor do I covet. Part of the problems with some who are *called* is their alliances with devils. These devils are hiding as you look around. Some are addictive behaviors others hiding in known faces. They are all over the place with bow ties and wrapped packages, disguised as a blessing from God. Becoming entangled with them sometimes leads to an untimely destruction.

As I come to the end of this chapter I want to leave you with the words of Apostle Paul in Romans 15:4, "For whatever was written in the earlier times was written for our instruction, so that through perseverance and encouragement of the Scriptures we might have hope." The stories of those before us must be the examples by which we follow. To persevere is to keep on trying and not quit, and as you push with courage know who has called you.

May you allow God to lead you in your *calling*; Be blessed.

Chapter 11

Faith and Its Walk

My definition of *Faith* is that, it is what we expect and the substantiation is unseen. I want to categorically state that if there is any great challenge in our walk as believers it is the walk of *faith*. Surprisingly I have come to know that some if not most men and women of God, claim to walk by faith (at their convenience), they also have faith if only they are guaranteed a check at the end of the month. Their faith is based on the tangible and well rooted and secured source. That my friends, is not faith; they are what I call 'the prepaid faith fakes' faith is to move to a place of the unknown, leaning only on God's promises, but having no guarantee or clear line in sight.

Two years in a row God woke me up with a revelation to go to a city called El Segundo, Ca. The reason for this city did not make any sense to me because the city is small, yet very strategically centered. The demography of El Segundo is Caucasian predominantly, considered by some as the Mayberry town in the South Bay area. My vision for the church is the one of God's rainbow of creation (multi-cultural), which is the image God has always shown to me and this image is not of the city. However, since they are His children and it is where He has called me to, He will make the way for His work to be done.

Both times the revelation came on the second week of each month. Both times the Lord pointed out specifically to a place between Aviation and Sepulveda, along El Segundo Blvd. The Lord showed men and women in the city in a building that was renovated and a podium was placed inside for me and these words were spoken to me, "whether they like it or not you are to stand here and preach." This building was like an old restaurant and had been for lease since 2005. The Lord said to me that these people have been praying for one like you and they are determined and swore that I must be there no matter the cost; they seek to see His church become a success.

Two years went by as I prayed and decided to visit churches in the El Segundo area to ask questions. I met one or two receptive pastors, and one in particular impressed upon me that my kind would have a difficult time fitting in there (and my answer to him was that I could care less because I am a child of God sent for His glory), but he felt I should join his congregation, and he actually said, "You are the one I had been praying for." To him there was no reason for me to start another church since his church is the one. But my answer to him was that God detailed me to the city and that I need to pray about his offer. The answer given by the Lord was that this pastor is too possessive of the church.

For two years or more now our church has been meeting in El Segundo in hotels praying and calling out on God. We are yet to see the fruition of the revelation, but we have steadfastly remained knowing that God will fulfill His promises. Regarding the vision of the building, we believe the Lord directed us to this building and we prayed and anointed the ground. We do not know how we can afford it but we know God will provide and make a way. And my friends in Christ guess what? That building is still listed on the market even as I write. Faith will always challenge you, and God will always sustain you if you remain steadfast.

I have decided that it is better to write this chapter on what *faith* and its walk is, than the totality of my challenges in the day-to-day journey. I do believe many have shared in this area with their own experience and some may have chosen to discuss what *faith* is as I am attempting to do here in this chapter. To live and walk in *faith* sometimes attracts ridicule, or worst humiliation at the hands of those that do not understand the journey in *Faith*. I have been called all sorts of names that one can imagine by those whom I have over the years past known. These performers may have come short of outright called me a thief. But their operation is one of self, and driven by the prince of this world (Satan). Some of these characters are nothing but mockers and detractors who must be overlooked because the battle is theirs with the Lord. My answer to them as the Psalmist said is directly from the bible in Psalm 109 and Psalm 35. They are nothing but the chaff and the tear that must be sift out of the wheat. We must remember that Jesus Christ was called worst John 15:18-20 speaks to kinds of hate and the rest of those who lived and walked by *faith* endured even greater pain and jumble. It is probably the reason that most people remain lukewarm in their *faith*.

In my circumstance God has held me back from acquiring employment in the secular realm. Pause and think about this for a moment… The response in the carnal mind of most is that this man must get a job, and frankly I have heard it. But when you are walking by faith and you know that God has spoken, you must obey! In our democratic society earning money is the means of our identity. But this is not always so in the life of God's *called* ones. We receive leadership and provision from the hand of the Maker. Does our time and in this society acknowledge or value the *faith* walk? The answer is no, because worth or the measure of humanity, is based on a paycheck.

And so, to live by *faith* and its *walk* remains out of the grasp of most people and sometimes unattainable by Christians. To be more accurate in biblical definition it states in Hebrews 11:1, "Now Faith is the substance of things hoped for, the evidence of things not seen." This definition reveals a part of life that is uncertain and unknown and in my walk it has actually been a journey. Yet because *faith* is in hope and that hope is in God, we who abide in Him our conviction is certain at the end; even though the evidence is presently unknown, this is the true essence of the meaning of *faith*. The joy here is that this hope is in God who is the almighty. He is the assurance of our faith, for all power is rested in His hands, the one who makes all impossibility possible. The ways of God are indeed not like the ways of humanity, is a statement that most may not understand the full capacity of.

To be *called* is to allow God to take us through those parts of life that are unknown. *Faith* therefore extends us, and strengthens us, in ways that we could never have imagined, helping in bringing us to that place of a true believer; which is to rely, depend, and trust in God.

Despite the confirmations of the call, the prophecies, the miracles, the dreams and visions, the walk by *faith* and in *faith* for me has been a grueling, humiliating, and even a painful journey. Brothers and sisters in Christ, to walk in *faith* causes you to become naked in a sense, stripped of every cover of pride. It brings you to a place of vulnerability leaving deep wounds and scars. It takes the grace of God for the hurt to mend. And lastly, you are hung on the balcony of ignominy and it is the place most of us are challenged in finding ourselves. I have found myself in this place many times in this walk of *faith*. I do not know when it will be over nor if it will ever be. However, like Paul, I am stretched in every corner, challenged by the norm of the society that insists if economically it is not rewarding, then throw in the towel. One thing that is certain is that God is holding me up including my family. Even when we are so pushed there is His voice that never makes sense to the norm that says, stand and know that 'I Am with you.' Another of the many things about *faith* is that you are never sure what is to come and how what has come can be managed. It is situation by situation, minute by minute, with the hope that everything will be alright tomorrow.

While through the grace of God I am determined to walk this journey of *faith* to the glory of our Lord because I am commanded to, many a night my tears continue to fill the bottle. According to the psalmist in Psalm in 56:8, "Thou tellest my wanderings: put thou my tears into thy bottle; are they not in thy book"? My suffering at the end is knowing that my God will ultimately justify me. And indeed the mighty hand of God continues to vindicate me.

I do know that somewhere around this world others have dealt or may very well be dealing with a more difficult situation in their various walks of faith, but to me this statement may be an under statement at best. In the U.S. it has been eight to ten painful years without a substantive income, lackluster church growth, prevented from securing any secular work, and yet commanded to stand and know that He has *called* me. Now and then gifts from some faithful saints and family members come. I have endured a mockery of sort from those that do not understand the walk of faith. Yet, through the support of my wife, my mother, children, and family members and their chairing of me in this journey, I have been encouraged in so many ways to push on and am ever so grateful. I have previously written about the dangerous effect of the denominations to the church. Part of the work that these groups have done over the years is to assist a segment of the people who wanted to work in the ministry whether professional or some called who have faced these challenges and some who are not willing to face these challenges in the areas of faith to starve off some of these experiences. But to each and everyone, his or her own, for we all must give an account of the race we have run.

I have indicated the dangers of expediency in faith and it is the reason that my determination is to do this work by His grace to the glory of God. Drawing to a close in this chapter my dedication in this book was to my late father who modeled for me what living by faith and walking in it was all about. I also know that it states clearly in 2 Thessalonians 3:2 "not all have faith." There are some among us who are not equipped to walk by faith.

Yet also, realizing that Galatians 3:23-25 tells us that faith is come to us through Jesus; Ephesians 2:8 "it is the gift of God." This makes it clear that Faith is a divine gift that is supernaturally given to some; so for anyone who may not understand it, I have been given a gift that overwhelms me sometimes. It is why I take issue when dealing with men and women of calculated manipulation in the ministry. These are people who think they have to use whatever method to achieve their ministry goal. If one calculates what they do and when it makes sense and sees that it benefits their own interest then there is a trouble for such are hardly led of God.

This will bring me to teaching on *faith* in our churches and at our schools. Can we truly understand the faith-walk from a man or woman with head-knowledge about faith and yet never personally lived through faith and walked in it? If anyone would have a problem in answering this question I will be bold to answer it for you the reader, the answer is No. We can only give what we have; giving what you do not have is to deceive the one you are giving to, a gift which at the end is no gift to begin with. At the top of this chapter I gave the scriptural reference about *faith* as a gift from God. I also mentioned my late father's model of *faith* living and *walk*. These two key truths are part of what makes me the man of *faith* that I am.

My legitimacy to write on this issue is based on my knowledge of the Word and its application in my personal life experience of *faith* here and now. Having the knowledge that not all are equally equipped or have the ability to walk by *faith*, it is therefore harder to accept one who has never walked by *faith* to teach others how they should live by *faith*. Again, I am a bona fide writer on this topic because in writing as with the rest of this book I have lived by *faith*. Summarized in the words of my late father who died in 2007, he would always say this, "in my prayer for you before the Lord, Uche my son, I am asking the Almighty God to lift up His foot off your head and bless your life (with ease) for you are not Job."

My deeper abiding faith has over the years grown stronger and developed as the revelations of God's truth have been made known to me. It is therefore upon this *faith* that my hope is rested in, in every way.

May you learn to walk by *faith,* and not by sight of what is in the present.

Chapter 12

Two or Three Gathered in His Name

Jewish tradition held that there must be ten people gathered for the synagogue to hold public prayers. Jesus established a new order in this regard, breaking the old Jewish rule. This is reflected in Matthew 18:20, "For where two or three have gathered together in my name, I am there in their midst." Jesus promises His presence in the midst of a smaller (flock) number for the purposes of discipline or prayer. In Mark 6 we read that the disciples were sent out in pairs; the in-house churches established in the New Testament by Apostle Paul and others began with smaller numbers. We do not read of too many places where they gathered in large numbers. This was the form of the beginning of the Christian movement, the disciples were sent out by two but it began with twelve and they for awhile were just eleven in number, before Matthias and then Apostle Paul much later.

Our church has found ourselves in this situation of walk of faith with two or three gathered in His name many times over. We have not being an exception to this rule. We started in my one bedroom apartment with few numbers. Over the years we have seen the flow of God's people, the coming and going, staying and leaving. God has given this prophecy, "many have walked away from you, but when they come back be reconciled." The promises were 'we are coming' and the visitors that pop in here and there. We as well have seen ourselves move from one house of worship to another, one hotel room to another. It is the journey in the work and walk of faith.

I wondered why it is so difficult for the church of God to grow in this society. I have friends who have five to fifty thousand member churches and some less, outside this country. What is it Lord? I know you have given me the vision to go to other nations of the world, if I am the problem would you Lord in the name of Jesus take *your* church into another hand. Anguished and crying out to God about His church the Lord decided to take me on a spiritual journey comprising of five to seven churches. One after the other the Lord swung open the churches doors to show me how empty His houses of worship are. Of the seven only about two had a considerable or significant number of people.

The lord took me to the larger of the two. He said, "You see the music, the dance, the crowd," and I said yes, Lord. He said, "But I am not there." Then he took me inside the smaller of the two and on the inside of the house with same scene of praise and dancing going on the Lord said to me, "do you see." I said, yes Lord. He said, "But I am not with them."

The Lord would proceed to take me back to other smaller churches and He said they are worshiping my name, and then upon returning to our place of worship, the Lord said, "now you stay here and continue to do what you are doing for I know you by name and I know what I am doing with you." At this point the Spirit or the Lord disappeared.

For years now I have had the opportunity of visiting and preaching from smaller churches of five to five hundred members in the U. S. and International of a much larger crowd the same way I preach to three to five. I compelled by necessity and led by the Holy Spirit to preach the same, no matter the size of the crowd.

Yet there are some who can only preach the Word of God if the number is large (Of course we know these characters are about money) but what does the Word of God teach us? That where 2 or 3 are gathered in His name there in their midst our Lord is. I have had some friends who for years have had sleepless nights over their church growth. Some have flown frequent mileages with the meager resources to attend some kind of a seminar here or there on how to grow their churches, and have come to terms with the fact stated in Psalm 127:1, "Unless the Lord builds the house, they labor in vain who build it." A well known brother in the Lord, a pastor, told me that the Lord spoke to him paraphrasing, 'that when you finishing running around I will show that I am the one who builds my church.' And he said to me, "since then I stopped running after people and focused on praying more and I have seen the Lord add to my church daily."

Saints of God I understand all the reasons behind it all, but gaining the world to loose your soul is pathetic. God is the one who brings the increase to His house and when He does they will stay. In the book of Acts the church was added to by the move of the Spirit. We have to learn to allow God to lead us in His work instead of us trying to manipulate our way into position of favor by tithing and we call it church.

Please know that I believe in tithing and we are a tithing church. It is a commandment that every believer must hearken to if they claim to be a believer. One thing I know is that the blessings of God in His time are all that matters, and it will also be enduring.

Would I have loved to have as many members as some of my brothers and sisters in faith? The answer is yes. But not in competition or in jealousness, for each one of us has our assignment and it is fulfilled at an appointed time. We must realize that all are not called in the same manner, and not all will shepherd a large church.

Many have gone to copy models of how others have been blessed with a large ministry only to find themselves in a confused state because they are chasing after chaffs blown-up in the wind (what is not theirs). I stand not against our learning from each other in the positive sense of the word through encouragement and exhortation but it should not be the evil of covetousness and envy for such is demonic. We fail to appreciate the fact we are nothing without God. The purpose for the *called* is having God be glorified as we genuinely affect the lives of His people through His leading, bringing the increase into the body, we call the church.

Find comfort in His presence outside the physical presence of others.

Chapter 13

The Gifts of God

Sitting to listen to a bishop who I have come to respect a great deal, a mockery of sort was made as he talked about one who was gifted as an apostle. In his own jest it went like this," I don't know what they call themselves now whether apostle, or whatever." He draws laughter from his adoring crowd as he clothed his disapproval of modern day apostleship, with his wit. I sat there in disbelief in the crass of this statement and the ignorance. It must be that cerebral cultural impediment that causes some people especially those in the West, to deny what is Spiritual even when it is Scriptural. What is the reason for this, I ask. In all accounts this is a well-lettered man. Does it mean that he does not see the order of the Spiritual gifting in the bible, or because his office has colored his sensibility. Later I will write on the office of the bishop, which is not one of the operations of Spiritual gifts, and their standing in the bible.

It is true that the dispensationalist would want us to believe that what God did by using a group of people (the Israelites) to tell his story on earth, should be confined to them and that time. And then some of the denominations claim that everything about gifts ended after Jesus. But the bible makes it clear that it is not so. One reason we know gifts still exists is that without them the church would not exist. There are still healings and supernatural manifestations from all corners of the world. Can we agree that there are still evangelists yet deny there are apostles?

Now back to the office of spiritual gifts in the bible, we know that Jesus in Luke 6:13 called His first disciples as the apostles, and then we see the biblical references of the order of the offices with Apostle Paul writing in 1 Corinthians 12:28, "And God has appointed in the church, first apostles, second prophets, third teachers, then miracles, then gifts of healings, helps, administrations, various kinds of tongues." Ephesians 4:11-14 states,

And He gave some as apostles, and some as prophets, and some as pastors and teachers, for the equipping of the saints for the work of service, to the building up of the body of Christ; until we all attain to the unity of the faith, and the knowledge of the Son of God, to a mature man to measure of the stature which belongs to the fullness of Christ.

These two texts define the office of spiritual gifts which Paul defined after the time of Jesus. It is important to note that Paul was called 'after' Jesus' ministries here on earth. I say this to point out that the office of apostle is not limited to those who walked with Jesus. Various denominations have to a great degree distorted and to some degree confused some lazy minded people whose biblical understanding is fulfilled by social belonging rather than studying the Word for themselves, and seeking God.

I hereby will tell two stories of how lazy some have become. I was at a Christian bookstore, what I had gone there for I cannot remember. But it was a store in Torrance, Ca. and all I heard was the end of the conversation of the store attendant saying, "Any time I hear anyone call themselves an apostle I do not go near them or their church." First, it caused me to laugh because she does not know the scriptures. Secondly, it saddened me because she probably never researched this on her own but was repeating what she had heard.

This other story was about a going-home funeral of a servant of God of whom I never knew while he lived, but God stirred my spirit to go. The reason for my attending this funeral was made manifest after

I had attended. Saints of God you will be blessed if you will hearken to God even when you don't understand the reason behind it. The people who gathered for the funeral were the rainbow of God's creation (all races), yet predominantly Africans. The master of ceremony was an excited young preacher from Ghana. In his introduction and in their style of doing things he called out all spiritual offices of gifting for convocations and believed that the office of the bishop was in his bible to be before that of an apostle. I refused to go forward and few friends that knew me asked why I was not going out. I told them the order of offices was distorted. For the office of the bishop is not among the spiritual gifts in the bible, respectively so to all who are called bishops.

I want also to state that my writing on this is not to say that some bishops are not *called* or anointed men and women of God, but in an earlier chapter I made it clear that due to denominational influence some have settled even when they know that is not their *calling*. What then is bishop? A bishop is an administrator, an overseer, a caretaker of surrounding smaller churches. The qualification is laid out by Apostle Paul in Titus 1:7-10. Apostle Paul is the one who originated the office of bishop in Acts 20:17, and in v. 28 he gives the title of bishop.

In the Catholic denomination the bishops are placed in position of authority in charge of ordinations. A bishop is an office that man can confer on another man. But not the office of an apostle for they are *called* by God as his special messengers for the entire body of the church, not confined to any particular local, state, or country. An apostle often operates in the five-fold gifting; they do the work of an evangelist, prophet, pastor and teacher. In the present time we hear that some even now announce themselves as an apostle - it is utter nonsense. All apostles before us were called by God; not self appointed.

An example of man appointing an apostle can be found in Acts 1: 15 -26; through the urging of Apostle Peter the apostles cast lots because they wanted to fill the spot left when Judas died. The lots fell on a man called Matthias but you do not hear much about him again after this. Jesus Christ *called* one Himself in the person of Apostle Paul and we read today what God did through his life. Saints of God only He calls people to Himself, and especially the office of an apostle.

Know that He is still calling-out His own.

Chapter 14

Preachers and Teachers of Correctness

To be a change agent is to be inimitable and it is only when that exclusivity touches the neutral that change occurs. The idea that Christianity must be like the rest of the societal context does not work. What do I mean? We Christians can not transform the society we live in when we are too busy compromising with the world. Concession cannot convert because to convert means that the person you are intending to convert must see something in your life that they are attracted to. If Christians are the same as the rest of the people in the world in appearance, attitude, and character, chances are that our uniqueness becomes irrelevant.

Preachers and teachers, what is the instruction we are given? We are commanded to transform the world. For us to do this we must be unashamed of the Gospel of Jesus Christ and be who we have been called to be with boldness, without needing to be liked by the rest of the people. There is nothing wrong in identifying with others, but our ways of life and who we are, must be identified with Christ foremost. Preachers, pastors, and teachers of the Gospel, a question I must pose to you is simply this, does it make sense to be right for the wrong reason? Choosing to be right for the wrong reason reveals the hollowness of a man or a woman without a Godly foundation. We should never dismiss God's commandments in order to please humanity or mankind.

In writing this chapter I am reminded of a professor who was a vexation to be frank, for what I know about him. He was one of those who felt every spirit is the spirit of God. Yes, he was teaching this in the seminary, a place that in all intended purposes was to prepare future shepherds of the house of God. In one of our many opposing views this was one of his cultural context off-loads to the students. He stated that the church does not need pastors; rather it should be a place where people gather to read and share stories because that is where the world is headed to. I was thunderstruck myself. Rhetorically I asked him why we need seminary professors. Why was it not okay for every student to read and award their degrees without a professor? He was upset and this nonsense is part of the thinking that is permeating the walls of some of our seminaries, and what has contributed to the malaise that is found in the church.

Also, there are preachers and teachers who think that dressing-down like most in the society are the key to attracting new members. Others think just call me panky, forget about my title 'we just be cool.' We're all equal so it is not about the title, they say. Their thinking in this regard is that their casual attitude makes them loved and acceptable thereby friction is avoided. They then wonder why they are not respected in their church. This attitude is pervasive today in the body of the church especially in our Western culture. Traveling through the streets of Southern California I saw a building where church is held and their sign fed on the carnal, Las Vegas slogan saying, "what happens in Vegas stays in Vegas." Do they know that they are saying, "You can come here in your sin and no one will know?" Another of their slogan was "a place for people that do not go to church, go to." In other words, if you do not like church, we offer a comfortable counterfeit.

A pastor I have known for a while thought the greatest card that defined his humility was, 'just call me by my first name,' until he realized that no one in his congregation respected his position as a pastor. I told him that he had brought it on himself and advised him to set boundaries and a rule, demanding henceforth it is unacceptable to be called by his first name; rather he should be addressed as pastor.

Months went by until he acknowledged how it changed the order in his church, yet his desire to be liked continues to keep him enslaved into egalitarianism thinking.

From politicians to police officers earthly authority is recognized and respected more than the office of a priest or pastor because of our lack of respect and knowledge about the things of God. People will buy a tuxedo just to go to the white house, they will dress in a tuxedo to go to a dog show, dress up every day to go to work, and to the bar to poison themselves with liquor, and yet we encourage them to come to church in shorts and beach sandals and we wonder why the church is ineffectual in changing lives.

When the bible said come as you are, I am sure that the hermeneutical understanding of that command is something other. I believe that it means come as you are broken on the inside, humbling yourself before the Lord to receive healing. Am I in any way suggesting that the poor without good clothing can't come to church? Not at all. I am not proposing that a homeless man without good clothing cannot attend the church; not in the least. You come with your best. There is order in all things and that includes how we come on Sunday morning. This part of thinking is the trend of egalitarianism mind-set, but with God there has always been hierarchy.

We read how Moses entered the tabernacle and all rose to their feet out of respect and remained standing until he took his seat. Jesus Christ walked with the apostle but there was no misunderstanding that He was the *Master*. Understand preachers and teachers that I am not talking about ego or being prideful, the hand of God is on my life. He has humbled me and continues through the enabling grace of God to kill my flesh daily. There is a reason why you are *called* to the position you are called if you're *called*, and that name you must wear to the glory of the one who has called you. Your parents gave names to you and that name was your mark of identity. You answer those names don't you? You did not grow up being called Mr. and Mrs. No Name, and the name given by your parents is not greater than the one God has *called* you. To own who you are is to be who that person is.

So please, by the grace of our Savior, stop this political correctness of the world and stand to accept whom God has *called* you. Move away from this nonsense of just call me winky.

Writing this chapter I do realize that some pastor's lack in the area of self-esteem and many may choose to remain in denial but the truth is that accepting how God called you is what will make you free. Your job is not to please the crowd but affect their lives with the truth that makes them free. There is nothing that should cause you to deny God in order that you might please humanity, it should not even be for the notion of entertainment or to avoid discomforting others with the truth. If most of us claiming to serve God are walking with integrity in our roles, the Church would be a place of respect and integrity. The weakness of the church is due to the lack of conviction in the likes of the 21st Century Christians and their compromises void of that integrity found in Paul.

Paul took charge and faced challenge in almost every scene you can find him in (Galatians 2:11-14). Paul confronts Peter against hypocrisy (1 Corinthians 11). While Paul did not invent the truth, he hands new and established Christians truths through his apostolic teaching.

This morning while writing a bit before my Sunday services I came across a song by a young Nigerian Gospel singer called Joe Praiz/Pace. It is a track on his compact disc that talks about how the love of God makes him shine like this, and how His love makes him glow like this. I ask that you join me and pray that the love of God will cause you to shine and glow in the mighty name of Jesus. For no one having experienced God's true love denies who God has *called* them to be. Humility is not found in rejecting who you are; and to reject is to refuse to accept what you have been *called*. Humility is the state of being humble. You can still humble yourself and not be arrogant or haughty. But to deny the position you are called is to declare yourself untrue. No one in the bible denied who they are *called* in order that they might please Him. Jesus never denied his role or rejected who

His father is. He walked bold and had no problem cursing-out those whom he felt were contrary to the will of his Father.

The meekest man called Moses according to the biblical history never denied who he was either. He was unassuming yet bold in every way as a man, and accepted his position of authority. Let us remember in all we do that we are nothing without the Father. I leave you in this chapter with this Scripture in 2 Corinthians 5:21, "He made Him who knew no sin to be sin on our behalf, so that we might become the righteousness of God in Him." It is my prayer that you experience the love of God if you have not yet experienced it in your life, and become unashamed of who you are *called* in Him.

May you be found in His grip; Amen

Chapter 15

Part 1: There is Something You Did Not Put There

I thought through the various parts my personal journey in my *calling* with God and considered that this book title will again reveal to the reader the rich wonders and goodness of God's grace. His gracious kindness is indeed overwhelming and I am ever so humbled by His hand in my life. How God can look down into the deepest valley and choose a sinful man like me fraught with weakness engulfs me, and forever I be bowed down in glory and adoration of Him. I have been married now to my wonderful wife Deborah for eight years. Before this union I was married to the mother of my beautiful teenage daughter, Adarundah (or Adandah).

In my previous marriage we experienced four miscarriages and a still born. I never can tell the reason why those experiences happened neither do I think that she can. Except that such disappointment and painful events occurred in the course of our time together. A gifted woman in Prophecy Evangelist Lizzy gave me a prophecy some time between 1996 and 1997 this she said to me, "You have been *called* by God; the wife you are presently with is not the one to go through this journey with you. She is not the wife for you but no matter what you do there will be a child between both of you. At the end of this marriage God is asking me to tell you that you should not look for another wife hence you make another mistake for your next wife, He will bring her to you." This was a message that would challenge and trouble most people, and I was indeed troubled and confused. I thought "he who finds a wife finds a good thing and obtains favor from the Lord" according to Proverbs 18. In the end I had no choice but to heed to God's message and warning.

It was a few years down the road before the marriage came to an end which to me was no longer a surprise but God's prophecy coming true. It was another seven years before Deborah and I became that unlikely couple *chosen* for His Glory. This was for me seven years of celibacy. I was holding fast to the warning of God and it became like a ringing bell-tone in my ear. It was by His enabling power that I was able to walk-it-through. Without Him I could not have made it. In this place in my life I had offers to marry-up or down. Pastor friends began to try and chose a wife for me. I saw those whom I thought were of the right quality (or so I thought).

Within this period I was blessed to manage a company store with over five-million dollars of inventory. In one case a mother whose daughter is a Ph. D. holder and currently a dean of a local college, had tragically lost her husband. She was in so many ways presented to me by the mother. All through this period the warning of God was like an alarm bell ringing out these words, 'He was to bring that wife to me'.

I was completely gripped with the fear of not making another mistake. I kept on crying out to God and at some point reminding Him that I was not gifted in celibacy (which now I think God must have been laughing out loud). Years went by and I went through an in-house bible college for three or four years. I was relieved of my duties as a minister for one year because of my divorce, and eventually became licensed a year later in ministry. I had been serving in ministry, volunteering at missions, preaching and teaching. I planned to start a home bible study group in preparation for a church launch as the Lord spoke and others brought their confirmation, but before this materialized I lost my place of residence.

Embarking on a search for a new place and not knowing the right direction to the manager of the complex, my arrival culminates with meeting a woman called Deborah for the first time in my life. I needed direction and she was kind in directing me to the manager called Audrey. I saw Deborah to be an attractive lady and never thought much of it nor was I sure to ever meet her again. By 2001 I secured tenancy in the complex with my daughter only three years of age. I was a single father managing a company, serving in huge church as a minister. I was a very busy man.

Late 2002 I called for the start of what would become my church plant, The Bible Church of His Will. I called friends and acquaintances I have known to attend which included Deborah, whose daughter would eventually babysit my daughter, but Deborah snubbed my invite. Disappointed I moved on. I believe it was the third or fourth meeting when she finally showed up. This became how both of us became acquainted with each other and other members.

As we began to fellowship Deborah was not very comfortable because of the viewpoint of her father, who was living at this time, further discouraging her by calling the gathering a cult. But she summed up courage and started attending. One thing that became comical was my three year old daughter who seemed to have taken to Deborah, performed this mock wedding ritual after the bible studies as we would gather to break bread together. She would always lift my hand or that of Deborah at one point or the other she would say, "dad would you take Deborah to be your wife." We all would laugh at it, I in particular never attached much meaning nor did I think Deborah did.

My ordination ceremony brought my sister, Florence, to attendance from Utah. Upon her return back she called to tell me that she thought Deborah would be the wife for me. My answer to her was that she did not posses what it took to be my wife. Looking back I came to realize that my answer was laden in arrogance and pride, but immediately my sister was to have none of it. In rhetorical question she asked, "Don't you think if God called her to be He will give her what it takes?" I was flabbgasted at her come back.

About a year would pass or two, a revelation from God came to me of Deborah in a seven to eight story high building about to fall to her death. The angel of the Lord was in search of me for in the spirit and I was in Nigeria, my country of birth. What I saw was that angels came to Nigeria and asked that I should accompany them hurriedly to my new country, the United States, that Deborah was about to fall to her death and that there was none on earth to rescue her except me. And we raced down to the U.S.

Upon our arrival in the spirit I asked for her whereabouts. The angel told me, "Look up" and I did and all I could see at this point was Deborah hanging at the edge of a seven to eight story high building. My second question was, "how can I get her down when I have no way of reaching her." It was at this point that the angel lifted my right hand up which in the spirit, came out from my body and extended eight stories high. I was instructed by the angel to open my palm and Deborah stepped on to it and gently I returned her back to earth. Now, I had no understanding what this meant except thinking that maybe God was asking me to shepherd her. This revelation I shared with her and that was the end of it.

Moving on, I received another revelation which startled me because I had seen her in front of my home in the spirit and she was complaining that I was not paying attention to her. I woke up again troubled and could not make sense of this either.

Then came 2003 when I had traveled to Nigeria and while there in a prayer session with my dear friend Evangelist Lizzy, as I mentioned a woman gifted in prophecy (now bear in mind that all this while I have been asking and reminding God of His promises to single-handedly bring to me a wife), Evangelist Lizzy said to me, "Apostle, God said tonight I will make known to you who is to be your wife." Ok Lizzy, I said to myself and returned later to my home. That night it was exactly at 3.00 am I heard a voice that shouted, Deborah! I immediately woke up and was shocked at hearing this for you see, in my eyes she was not the quality of woman I was looking for or so I thought. This vain mind still had other thoughts and what they were was convoluted.

Immediately I went to my knees before God petitioning that I did not want to make a mistake and that I knew there was another woman named Debra who I had met. I told God that I needed Him to show me a picture of the actual woman called Deborah. The following day at exactly the same time of 3:00 am it was almost like God was saying to me, "You fool why you are messing with me?" I will let you know that, I AM WHO I AM. A huge screen appeared before my eyes about 64 inches wide and in it was a full body picture of Deborah and it froze for a moment before it disappeared.

This was a hard moment of truth for me. I cannot wiggle myself out of this. Upon returning to the United States I was mum. I never said a word to Deborah of the revelations, wishing that she would find her a man so that I can say to God she is unavailable. June or July of 2004 a defining moment occurred while I had travelled to Europe and Nigeria on a six week trip. I had the opportunity of fellowshipping with the evangelist once again in prayer. This night Lizzy gave me the prophecy of a lifetime as she said, "Apostle when you return to America there is something in your house that you did not put there. God is asking me tonight to tell you that whoever has put it there is the wife I have set apart for you."

Deborah had access to my place because in leaving the country I had given her my keys to pick up my mail. Two weeks later I returned into the United States. My taxi from LAX could not lip over the entire South Bay quickly enough to the Torrance area, in a small city called Lomita nestled between San Pedro a suburb of the greater Los Angeles and Long Beach. Arriving home I entered with my spare keys to my home. I was anxious this time to see what was inside my home that I had not placed there prior to leaving the country. As I arrived opening my door, I laid down my heavy winter coat on the chair close to the front door, thanking God for His protection over eighteen thousand miles of flight first and foremost.

I spoke to God in these exact words, "God while I was over ten thousands mile away you spoke through the mouth of your servant. Now I need you to show me what is in this house that I did not put here prior my departure. I began methodically in my survey inside the entire unit beginning from the kitchen area with cabinets first, to the living room, bathroom, the bedroom, and the walk-in closet, carefully checking out the few suits I had not taken, shirts, and pants; nothing strange was noted. I dropped down, took a peek under the bed and I could see nothing that was new. While I walked around in the house I was saying to Jesus, answer me for I see nothing.

I went back to the front door where I began my investigative search with all my suit cases sitting at the door, I said aloud, "God I know you did not lie to your servant Lizzy in Nigeria, and I know that you are not a man that you should lie, what is it in this house that I was to see?" Then I stood for a moment, quietly waiting to hear His voice then in a silent tone I heard in my spirit, "check in your kitchen cabinet." But I checked there already, I murmured to myself as I proceeded to open the same place I had opened and never saw anything. And ah! There it was a new set of cookware.

I fell to my knees with tears strolling down my cheek, I began thanking God for His Goodness and favor upon me, his servant, and then I began laughing and praising His Holy name. A day or two later I called Deborah who probably saw my lights but never bothered to call me upon my return to the country. Her answer was, "I had seen your light and knew you must be back." I mentioned the new set of cookware I saw in my house, and I asked what it was about? She said, "Oh' I had gone to Bed Bath and Beyond and there was a sale to buy one and get one free, and I thought you might make use of it."

Can you wait and trust Jesus to come to you before you leap.

Chapter 16

Part 2: There is Something You Did Not Put There

Not saying a word to Deborah about the prophecy, I continued with the work of ministry like nothing happened except for the tokens of appreciation that I had brought back from my travels to Deborah and other faithful members. But deep inside of me I felt different about her somewhat, and felt it was necessary to be interactive, after all my hand in marriage is hereto forced.

I believe it was a week or two later that I went to a pastor I had come to admire and respect. While seated in his office and charting about ministry and life (especially about another lady who really thought she was the wife for me and indeed she told me she will see it no other way than that she was the wife). Out of the blue this pastor asked how about his former church member (Deborah used to attend his previous church), and I asked who? He describes Deborah and said to me, "have you thought about her?" I asked why? He said, "No reason," being the cautious man that I had known him to be and he did not elaborate further.

Now this was just too much for me. I proceeded sharing with this pastor the prophecies and the revelations surrounding Deborah. Two days later with my deficiencies in the area of romantic formalities, I called Deborah at work and she was surprised since I have never called her at work. I asked if she had a moment that I had something to tell and ask of her. And she said yes, putting me on hold for a moment. Upon returning to the phone I said Deborah I have decided that you are the one I will marry. I still can hear the gasp and then she said to me, are you crazy? I said no, I am not crazy but God has called you to be my wife. Her next statement was, are you serious, how can I marry you when I have never even dated you? Yes Deborah, I said. And she said we can't talk any further let me think about this. I said okay and hung up.

The yes answer came a week later and on August 4, 2005 with a hand of people, four pastors, and one officiating pastor, Deborah and I entered into holy matrimony. This is how Deborah and I became husband and wife. Our wedding was a very simple one; we had the blessings of God but we had no money. When God is in your midst fellow soldiers of the cross, things that may mean much to an unbeliever is less to the life of a true servant of God. I must also applaud my wife Deborah who trusted in God most of all, in faith, and jumped into the deep ocean called the walk of faith; I could not be better blessed. *Thanks to Jesus.*

Listen to this, our wedding cake was from Costco, bought by a faithful servant of God called Father Duane. The refreshment was provided by him as well. It was quick and done with because it was only a handful of people. The gift that was given came from my mother-in-law who gave us $500.00 towards what was suppose to be a celebration at least for us a night or two at a hotel. Unexpectedly a church member had a need amongst us. Our church was small at the time and I suggested to Deborah that we needed to use the money to bless his life. Deborah was taken back by this request initially but she willingly agreed and we did. It has been eight years of marriage without a honeymoon or a vacation, but through the entire time the Lord has sustained us for His glory until one day we will take that honeymoon.

To many our marriage did not make sense but when God is leading the ways of a man or woman, their path will most likely be misunderstood. I remain ever so thankful to God for directing my path. I have been blessed with His hand-*chosen* servant and she is all that I could have ever asked for in a woman. Deborah is my friend, sister, and above all the wife God gave to this servant of His.

Our journey thus far has not been easy in the work of the ministry but we continue to trust God for we know that He who *called* us will not leave us, and thus far He has not forsaken us. May our story bring somebody who is struggling to obey God to hearken to Him, for it is easier to wait in obedience than to pay the price for disobedience, because that price will surely be great!

Be encouraged and know that your greatest joy comes when you wait on God

Chapter 17

Do We Know What is of God and What is Not?

The tragedy of life is that humanity can be foolish and choose to continue in foolishness. The denial of the existence of God's sovereignty by humanity, to will and not to will, is perplexing and totally reveals the veil of our ignorance as to who God is. Countless stories and events of how God dealt with those before remind us of the awesomeness of God. God's encounter with Balam and a Moab king called Balak in Numbers chapters 22- 24 should give humanity a pause. In chapter 22 the event of history begins with Balam, a man gifted in prophecy yet throughout the bible he was never referred to as a prophet.

Balam was a good man who never had the heart of God (meaning not a Godly man), and this good man is just what many are in the church and the seminaries today, sadly. They are so good at displaying the things that resemble God's goodness but their heart is fraught with self aggrandizement. The reader should note that even when God warned and instructed Balam not to curse Jacob and his people for they are blessed people, Balam was in disobedience and after self-gain which was his motivation for the continued pursuit in prying into a door that he was warned to keep shut. This behavior sadly is a practical example of what most preachers and teachers in our time are caught-up in. They walk in disobedience and reign falsehood.

God also caused the mouth of Balam to proclaim blessings on

Jacob and his people in the presence of Balak, who wanted them cursed to his hearing. This is how mighty the God we serve is. Sometimes brothers and sisters in Christ, God will use the wrong intention of the wicked as blessings to His blessed. God at the end was displeased with Balam and it cost him his life in Numbers 31:5.

This chapter is to remind us that the ways and the thinking of humanity are contrary to the ways of God. What is impossible to the human comprehension is all so right and possible with God, which brings me to ask the question, who can tell what is of God and what is not? If God can use the sight of a donkey to see, and the mouth to speak, as we read Numbers 22:23-30, is there anything God cannot do?

I wish to dispel the assumption of humanistic thinking whether in the seminary or outside the walls of it, where people believe the mind of God is bound. I say bound because humanity in their arrogance have delimited God. Even some Christian men and women who claim to know God assert, "This is not of God."

To a degree we can have the doubts and exercise our comparisons and study the things of God. But at the end we may realize that the work of God is beyond the seminary intellectual pursuit or any form of educational accomplishments. Rather it is the Holy Spirit who gives us the insight into the mysteries and secret knowledge of Him who has *called* us into this work of the ministry of service for His glory. It matters less how articulate the prayers are said, without the power of the Holy Spirit it is meaningless.

When we deny prophecies of those *called* of God are we not in danger of totally missing-out on who God is? I am not in anyway asking the reader to believe anyone who calls themselves a name, it is after all one of the reasons for this book, but the bible has warned and commanded us to test the spirit and it is now on you. In 1 Thessalonians 5:21 we are told to test all things; Hold fast to what is true.

The bible is full of instructions of who God is, and His Word encourages our hearts in perseverance to know that He is God, for us to have hope according to Romans 15:4. Still myopic and cerebral thinking on the things of God is causing us to wander as sheep.

We also read another example of how God moves in Isaiah 20:2-3 where His prophet was instructed to walk naked. This act was to show humiliation and disgrace against Egypt and Ethiopia in the hands of the Assyrians. Can any of the so-called educated fools of our time, in the church, and in our seminaries, not be the first to deny and denounce if such an event was in this present time.

Two or three chapter before in this book, I mentioned how God spoke of my divorce from my previous wife. You see the narratives of biblical accounts tells of things that were somewhat I thought a bit strange which happened with some individual lives, but never in my wildest dream did I ever postulate that I would be found around these events. What do I mean? That a child was to be born to me, no matter what I did, and at the same time God spoke His oracle through the mouth of His servant that I was ultimately to be divorced. Who has heard such a thing before? Is God not the same God that hates divorce? Are you sure this is from God and not from the devil? Saints of God these were all the questions that were going through my mind. (Indeed let truth be told according to His words God hates divorce, and I must add I will not wish divorce on anyone but it was not to stop Him from accomplishing His purpose with me for His glory…Oh, no). This is the grace of God that even when you blow it, His mercy is great towards us.

All this I was asking and I was thinking at the same time, and assuring myself that this must be of God, because I have known this woman and her gift of prophecy for a long time. She is an incredible gifted woman, one who speaks and her word comes forth. All the while I saw myself as an exception from the ways that God dealt with these characters that had gone before me; whether it is that of forbidding Jeremiah from marrying, or asking Prophet Hosea to go marry a prostitute for God's demonstration of His love.

For me at that moment it did not make any sense what I had been told. At this period and time those that were teaching had us believe that God was one dimensional with His works. So when I came to this place in my life and the strange revelation that was given to me, I was saying to myself, "what, this cannot be of Him." And my wondering continued in this way but at the end God did prove that He is God of yesterday, today, and tomorrow to come, because this account in my own life came to pass and I live to share it now in this book.

The New Testament and the accounts of the miraculous birth of Jesus Christ reveal something that in all confound the understanding of humanity. We for some reason have no choice but to accept it though I should attest that there are those who still cannot come to terms with the divine birth of Christ.

As I come to the final touches in writing this book, recently something happened in southern California, a tragedy that claimed innocent lives including some police officers this February at the hand of a former police officer. It was almost five or six days that the manhunt for him continued on high scale, with every community on the edge after some innocent people have been seriously wounded because the police officers had mistaken them for the renegade cop. Prior to this event, on the 9th or the 10th of February, the Lord gave me a revelation about the rogue cop. I had seen him in a white truck. On opposite direction of swat team there was a stand-off. He was commanded to exit his vehicle but he refused. He had sworn not to be taken alive. I saw him bending down to shoot himself on the right of his temple.

Now, this revelation was shared with some people, an attorney friend, a lady I had met at the gym called Thea, my wife as always, and in a laundry-mat I spoke to two guys about what the Lord had revealed would be the manner of death for the disgruntled cop. A man who calls himself a believer but thrives in the mockery of the prophetic things of the God, responded to me, "If you saw him kill himself, has the Lord shown you his body?" On this day at about 12:30 pm-6.00 pm the cop killed himself in a stand-off with the police.

The same week the Lord gave me a prophecy of a legend in the basketball industry and a franchise owner dying and that his funeral would be held at the stadium like that of Michael Jackson in downtown Los Angeles. I told my wife, an attorney friend, and a pastor I emailed to agree with me in prayer against such death but above all let God's will be done. These people are living to testify this truth. A week or less the owner of the Los Angeles Lakers lost his life. This is He whom we serve.

Our constancy to God cannot be continuative on fickleness rather we approach Him with self-effacing heartedness in honor of His awesomeness. When I hear people claim that they have relationship with God and equally on the same breath second guess the sovereignty of God, I see nothing but people with ephemeral walk. If we claim to know God or have relationship with Him, we in trepidation should not be too quick in the judgment of what is not of God. Brothers and sisters in Christ Jesus, God is greater than what we ascribe Him to be. My personal experiences in revelation, prophecy, dreams, and the miraculous experiences of our God through His grace, have shown me nothing short of His Omnipotent, Omnipresence, and the Omniscience. God has allowed me to experience great wonders for His glory and indeed it reveals that He is the "ELOHIM," the object of fear and reverence. As you seek to know Him, know that all is in His Hands

Are you still in doubt about who He is?

Chapter 18

The Person and the Works of the Holy Spirit

The reader should know that the aim of this chapter is to show that the Holy Spirit is a person, in the same sense that God the Father is a person. The Holy Spirit is not merely a floating spirit without purpose or direction but moves by the divine will of God. We will see how the Holy Spirit is weaved into creation and manifest in the success of lifting us beyond our degenerate life to eternal life in Christ. The problem is that few people truly believe the power of the Holy Spirit, much less understand who He is.

Theologians for centuries have had arguments and debates as to who the Holy Spirit is. One wonders why such debates, if our focus is centered on God who was the beginning before the beginning began. Simply put, the Scripture is plain in description of the person of the Holy Spirit. The error is when our understanding is filtered through human intellectual processes. The Holy Spirit is placed outside our realm of reason, so without the Holy Spirit directing out thoughts we will never truly know Him.

Some of such debates have been centered on those who have believed in the personality of the Holy Spirit and in His deity, even stressing the Trinity, yet have denied the individual distinct persons in the Godhead. They have argued that God made His ascendances differently, one at the time of the Father, the other as the Son and of course as the Holy Spirit in Godheads.

From the beginning it was clear that God made known the person of the Holy Spirit in Gen.1:2. In God's creative work the Holy Spirit's independence was established as revealed in Gen.1:2b. To define the Holy Spirit therefore, is to see the very character of God, the immutability, and the personality of God. The Holy Spirit is the third person in the Holy trinity, true God with the father and the son. He is not merely the power of energy of God as Judaism teaches.

This seems contrary to the accounts of events in the biblical history (Gen1:2b). Also Gen1:26 reads, "Let Us make man in our image, according to our likeness." This also implies that our image was not merely of a non-material being but of the personhood of the Holy Spirit. Human beings would have been referred to as "it" meaning that we would have existed with no emotions, neither could we as humans had been able to posses the very character of God in whose image we are made of.

In Eph. 4:30 we read, "Do not grieve the Holy Spirit of God." Can a non-being be grieved? Has any one seen or heard where a non-being had emotions or feelings? It therefore means that the Holy Spirit is a divine person. Many other scriptural references bring this debate to light as Packer would write, "Again the Holy Spirit is said to hear, speak, witness, convince, glorify Christ, lead, guide, teach, command, forbid, desire, give speech, give help, and intercede for Christians with inarticulate groans, himself crying to God in their prayers (John 14:26; 15:26; 16:7-15; Acts 2:4; 8:29; 13:2; 16:6-7; Rom. 8:14,16, 26-27; Gal., 4:6; 5:17-18). Also, he can be lied to and grieved (Acts 5:3-4; Eph., 4:30). Only of a person could these things be said. The conclusion is that the Spirit is not just an influence; He, like the Father and the Son, is an individual person."

What does the other religion say? Islam, Hinduism and Judaism say and teach this about the Holy Spirit; Islam considers the Holy Spirit to be another name for the archangel Gabriel. In the Quran Gabriel delivers the word of Allah to the prophet Muhammad. Gabriel is actually called "the Holy Spirit". They believe angels have no will of there own so they cannot disobey. In Hinduism the Holy

Spirit, referred to as Kundalini, is the divine intelligence behind spiritual awakening in Yoga. Judaism believes the Holy Spirit is for the Christians a concept. The Holy Spirit is not identified as a separate person, but as a Divine power which could fill men. This is however what the bible declares and what Christianity believes and knows about the Holy Spirit;

Jesus Christ promised us the Holy Spirit before His ultimate death on the cross. In John 7:38 Jesus states, "He who believes in me, as the Scripture has said, out of his heart will flow rivers of living water." John 7:39 tells us, "Those believing in Him would receive; for the Holy Spirit was not yet given, because Jesus was not yet glorified."

Every indication would point to the fact that until the death and resurrection of Jesus Christ there was not much mention of the Holy Spirit indwelling in the life of believers. However, the creative work was in evidence in His person. The Holy Spirit was noted in few places in the text such as Psalm 51:11 where David cried out for forgiveness. Isaiah 63:10 tells about the rebellion of the children of Israel. David's last word was in 2 Sam 23:2, "the Spirit of the Lord spoke by me, and His word was on my tongue."

An accurate definition of the Holy Spirit was made known also in Isaiah. Isaiah listed the role of the Spirit, "The Spirit of the Lord shall rest upon Him, The Spirit of wisdom and understanding, The Spirit of counsel and might, The Spirit of knowledge and of the fear of the Lord (Isaiah 10:2)." And Joel 2:28-29 tells about the Spirit. And in the book of Acts the outpouring of the Holy Spirit took place as it was first predicted.

In John 14:1-7 Jesus assures His Disciples and all believers of His departure and reminded us all that it is through Him that our relationship with the heavenly Father is realized. This particular phrase or statement is what I have always called the 'exclusive clause.' Some state differently and assert that there are other avenues to the most High God. Jesus Christ promises us of being joined again in glory (John: 14:16-18). The Paraclete, called the Spirit of Truth, was promised as His replacement which is the Holy Spirit. His job was to counsel, comfort and guide believers in the absence of Jesus.

There is no question in my mind neither should it be in the mind of any believer that the Holy Spirit's gift to us proceeded from the Father, through Jesus, for the equipping and regeneration of the believers. And it is in this stand I agree with Moltman when he writes,

> In the farewell discourses He is called the Paraclete, whom Jesus promises to His followers, whose coming he makes possible through his departure and pleads for in his act of self-giving. He is called the Spirit of truth or the Holy Spirit. He is the witness of Christ, who leads us to knowledge of the truth. He is one with the Son and the Father through the Son in those who belong to him. He is the giver of the eternal life of God to the world which has fallen victim to death. So when we say 'Pentecost is the *telos*, the highest goal of revelation in Christ', it is true as far as the gift of the Spirit is concerned; but if we are considering the fulfillment of the meaning of the history of Christ we also have to talk about the history of the Spirit.' For 'it is at the same time the beginning of the new time, the time of the direct and lasting presence of revelation in history.[15]

Without Jesus believers would not have the Holy Spirit. Believers are defined as those who belong to Him as stipulated in John 14:21, "He who has my Commandments and keeps them, it is he who loves me. And he who loves me will be loved by my Father, and I will love him and manifest myself to him."

What was the reason why it was necessary for Jesus Christ to send the Holy Spirit in His place? The answer is that after the fall of Adam, man in the depraved state necessitated the need for the Holy Spirit. God could not have allowed man in his unregenerate state;

---

15 Jurgen Moltman, *The Church in the Power of the Spirit*, (Minneapolis, MN: First Fortress Press, 1993), 34

hence Jesus' death became the Salvation for mankind that set us free from sin. Man was in need of righteousness and in perfect order of attainment; a new righteousness was to be, and the only way was for mankind to be born again with a new spirit of Jesus Christ through whom we became recipient of the Holy Spirit. This was the reason why Jesus Christ told a man called Nicodemus that he needed to be born again. Why, because he needed the Spirit of truth to guide him in service of God.

Even in the position of Nicodemus as a Rabbi, a teacher of the Jewish law, a new birth of the Holy Spirit through none other than Jesus, would be necessary. John 3:1-6 with particular emphasis on verse 5, this Jesus answered, "I assure you, most solemnly I tell you, unless a man is born of water and the Spirit, he cannot enter the kingdom of God."

Genesis 5:1-3 states, "In the day that God created man He made him in the likeness of God. He created them male and female, and blessed them and called them mankind in the day they were created. And Adam lived one hundred and thirty years, and begot a son in his own likeness, after his image, and named him Seth." We then read about the fall of man that made it necessary for Jesus Christ to send the Holy Spirit. When Adam sinned he no longer reflected the image of God. The Bible tells us that he was driven from the garden and the Cherubim were placed at the gate to prevent him from reentering. His fellowship terminated with God and was lost.

According to the biblical account we are descendants of Adam. The original state of man without sin was lost as Adam became scarred with the consequences of sin, so also was all mankind who followed. Jesus Christ would die for the sin of humanity in order to reconcile us with the Father, giving us a righteousness that was immaculate.

This became the order, granting us the ability to accomplish our worship unto God which is the purpose of our creation to begin with. Our heart and mind needed renewal. In the earlier chapter I stated that Jesus prayed to the Father to send us the comforter, counselor, teacher, strengthener, and the Spirit of Truth the person of the Holy Spirit to guide us in all things and in all truths. Hebrews states that the Holy Ghost is witness to the Word being placed in our hearts and in our minds.

As I alluded to earlier in the text, the Holy Spirit was known and was of first mention in the Old Testament. His works and Personhood are recorded in Genesis 1:2, Psalm 51:11, Isaiah 63:10, Gen1:26, Isaiah 11:2, Matt 28:19, the full outpouring of the Holy Spirit was not until Acts 1:2, Mark 1:23, 40-42, 2:1-12, Acts 2:2. In each of these Scriptural references of the presence of the Holy Spirit was made effect in the very actions that took place. How can we claim this to be true? The Holy Spirit was poured out on to the believers in Acts. In Mark the crowd was in amazement at the work and power of Jesus wondering what kind of a man that commands the evil Spirits and they obey Him. Another illustration was with the paralytic where Jesus through the Holy Spirit perceived the thought of the Scribes who accused Him of speaking blasphemies when the word out of Jesus mouth was spoken unto the paralytic, "Son, your sins are forgiven you."

A non-believer cannot claim the Holy Spirit because of what Jesus Christ had to say Himself in the Scripture in John 14:15-16, "If you love me, keep my commandments." Which means those who love Him will prove their devotion by their obedience. Then in verse 16, Jesus Christ said, "Then I will pray the Father, and He will give you another Helper that He may abide with you forever."

What does it mean then for the non-believer? It means that the Holy Spirit remains available and accessible to those who are willing to accept Jesus Christ and walk in the life of devotion by their obedience. How about a Christian who is in disobedience of the commandments of Jesus Christ? It simply means they have a choice to make to live a life that pleases the Lord or choose to remain vulnerable to the schemes of the devil. It is where the Holy Spirit is quenched and grieved rendering the counsel to fall on deaf ears and the truth of the Spirit un-adhered to.

What happens then to a Christian who walks in constant disobedience? It simply means that God may give them over to their own counsel, and the guidance of the Holy Spirit departs. A serious and committed Christian will not risk staying outside the counsel of Holy Spirit. One of the most puzzling aspects of God is His Grace in giving the Holy Spirit to Mankind. It is the undeserving love of God through His gift of the Spirit, known as unmerited favor. Edwin H. Palmer puts it this way in his book, The Holy Spirit, pg 29 "One of the least recognized, but one of the most far-reaching activities of the Holy Spirit is his uncommon grace. This consists of his restraining the reprobate to do good, and the instilling in the reprobate of certain abilities to perform cultural tasks."

It is the pure grace of God that gave mankind the Holy Spirit, while we were in a fallen state of depravity. With no goodness of our own, God through His love gave us the gift of the Holy Spirit for man's restoration. Man is utterly and completely lost without the Holy Spirit.

Palmer writes,

The natural man that is, the man without the supernatural working of the Holy Spirit in his life, does not in the basic sense know God nor truth. Although he seems to understand many things, he does not understand a single thing truly because he does not relate it to the God of the Bible. He should be able to know God by observing God's power and wisdom in the works of nature, but Romans 1:18 tells us that the natural man suppresses this truth, hinder it, holds it down in unrighteousness. In 1 Corinthians 2:14, 15, we read that "the man without the Spirit [or the natural man KJV] does not accept the things that come from the Spirit of God, for they are foolishness to him, and he cannot understand them, because they are spiritually discerned. [16]

The Bible reminds us that the very heart of man is deceitful and

---

16 Edwin H. Palmer, *The Holy Spirit: His Person and Ministry*, (Baker Book House Company 1958),30

desperately wicked Jeremiah (17:9). We are also warned in Gen (6:5) that in a continuous state of wickedness are our intensions.

Everywhere one looks in and through the Bible can read of the weak, inept and wicked state of man as it is ever so present before us. John (15:5) says we are nothing without Jesus Christ. In Romans (3:10-1 8) we read that there is none amongst us who loves God. We seem not to have fear of God in our heart. All that can be wrong with man Paul listed in this very passage referenced above about humanity and their waywardness.

Amongst those who are called Christians it would appear that sometimes we are more swiftly to anger and wrought with evil intentions than unbelievers. Other times it would appear that there are people who are givers rather than takers all through their life. There are men and women who devote their entire life for the good of their fellow mankind; how do we explain this? We read the hopeless description of man in what some have accepted to be the perfect good in man. But if we are to accept the Bible as the infallible word of God, we must believe what the Bible says and realize that the work of grace through the Holy Spirit is at work in our lives. A good example in my own life is that there have been many situations where I saw myself headed towards deep waters that even would have ruined my life for good, before I made a decision to serve God. It was nothing but the undeserving unmerited grace of the Holy Spirit.

According to Torrey, Jesus told the disciples before he left to be with the Father, "Behold, I send the promise of my Father upon you; but tarry ye in the city of Jerusalem, until ye be endued with power from on high" (Luke 24:49). The promise of the Father was that they would be baptized in the Holy Ghost not many days hence. The book of Acts (1:8) tells us that they will receive power after the Holy Ghost would come upon them. [17]

It was not enough that they trained with Jesus for three years. This is an example of the importance of receiving the baptism of

---

17 R.A. Torrey, *The Person and Work of the Holy Spirit,*(United States of America, Whitaker House 1996),215

the Holy Spirit before we minister to the lost. Any Christian who is involved in ministry should follow the principle in Luke 24:49 "Tarry ye [sit down] until ye be endued with power from on high." Just hear this fellow saints, sit down and wait. This is the instruction, if it is too late for you; it is never too soon for God. At the appointed time if you are called you will be endued with the power for the work to which you have been called.

The Holy Spirit work of creation began in Gen (1:2) though the Word used was the *Spirit* He was the Holy Spirit. In Gen1:26, God said, "Let us make man in our image."

As Edwin H. Palmer writes in The Holy Spirit; His Person and Ministry, pg 22, "With these Trinitarian distinctions as a background for our thinking, we may now proceed to see what the Bible says more directly about the work of the Holy Spirit in creation." The story in the Bible introduces the basis for the Holy Spirit in conjunction with the Father and the Son in creation (Gen 1).

According to the work of Walvoord, "The first reference to the Holy Spirit is in the scene of darkness and chaos described in Gen 1:2. The Spirit of God is revealed to have "moved upon the face of the waters."[18] It is interesting to read that Holy Spirit, which is also known in the description of a dove, was hovering upon the face of waters before the night and the day definitions were made.

The work of creation with the Holy Spirit was methodical; a work that the human intellect in all its advances has yet to figure out. Maybe I can say, that it was not made for the human understanding. In the words of Palmer, " Notice that as in the creation of the world the Holy Spirit did not create out of nothing, but gave life, order, and beauty to a dead, inert, dark earth that was waste and void by "brooding over the face of the waters."[19] The work of the Father with

---

18 John F. Walvoord, *The Holy Spirit: A Comprehensive Study of the Person and Work of the Holy Spirit*, (Van Kampen Press, 1954), 37

19 Edwin H. Palmer, *The Holy Spirit: His Person and Ministry*, (Baker Book House Company 1958), 27

the Holy Spirit remains one of the wonders of human existence that defy our imagination.

Job 26:13 portrays the beauty of the dove as it says, "By His Spirit He adorns the heavens." Now none of us have seen the heavens, but isn't it an awesome feeling to gaze at the sky to see the beauty of the moon, sunset, and the sunrise. How often have we gathered to watch the eclipse? What a perfect work of God we all admire with gaze.

Psalm 19:1 speaks about the revealed light of the Spirit. It talks about the declared divine work as a completed work that is to bring glory to God. It says, "The heavens declare the glory of God; and the firmament shows His handiwork." There is so much that can be said about the work of the Spirit that it is infinite.

Psalm 104 bears out another aspect of the creation of the Holy Spirit in life giving of the trees, fishes of the sea, birds of the air and the animals. The psalmist here brings to mind the beauty of nature. Are the things of nature fascinating to mankind? We all can acknowledge with an Amen. We are enamored with animals today in our contemporary world, especially in the west where the ownership of some pet to some is the measure of humanity, not that I ascribe to it, nor do I condemn any but at least that is what it appears to be. Psalm 33:6 again makes the focus of the perfecting work of the Holy Spirit we read, "By the word of the Lord the heavens were made and all the host of them by the breath of His mouth." For it is with breath and the dust of the ground that mankind became a living being (Gen1:27).

The Holy Spirit is seen as a dove that was witnessed by John the Baptist as the Spirit descended on Jesus Christ in (Luke 3: 22); "And the Holy Spirit descended in bodily form like a dove upon Him, and a voice came from heaven which said, "You are my beloved son; in you I am well pleased." Part B of this quotation has few theologians in doubt whether it was really a voice or an old Jewish expression. For me it is not hard I can tell and agree with the bible narration of event when it states "A voice came from heaven." I have heard similar voices in messages and instructions in my journey with the Lord with

His grace. Why it is easy to doubt by some is because to some if not many, there is no spiritual experience beyond the natural existence of humanity. What is the significance of the dove and meaning? The dove represents to us the sign of peace, gentility, beauty and care.

The Holy Spirit arriving on the day of the Pentecost is described as a mighty rushing wind in (Acts 2:2); "And suddenly there came a sound from heaven, as of a rushing mighty wind, and it filled the whole house where they were sitting." The earliest work of the Holy Spirit in the New Testament gives examples of Christ moving in the power of the Holy Spirit. In Mark 1:23 casting out demons, 2:1-12 Jesus heals a paralytic, 1:40-42 Jesus healed a leper, 1:29-34 Jesus healed the sick of various diseases); Why in Mark? Why not the other Gospels? Because even though the writer of the Gospel of Mark was anonymous, early tradition is unanimous that the author was John Mark, a close associate of Barnabas and Paul on their first missionary journey (Acts 12: 25)

We are all instruments of the Holy Spirit. Without the cooperation of Christians, the Holy Spirit could not reach unbelievers or the church in the present. In order to be used by the Holy Spirit we must be willing to set aside our own desires and go after the success that God has assigned us to. First in becoming who we are in Christ and second, doing what we are called to do. We must be baptized by the Holy Spirit to achieve the commission given to us by none other than our Lord.

The most important reason for sending the Holy Spirit is for us to reach the lost in the world with the good news of salvation. In order for the Word to spread there must be leaders who are chosen of the Holy Spirit and led by Him, not by the program of man's schema. Matthew 28:18-20 says, "Go therefore and make disciples of all the nations, baptizing them in the name of the Father and of the Son and of the Holy Spirit." When Christ's work was finished on earth, the Holy Spirit was given to us for His assignment on earth. The Holy Spirit guides and leads the hearts of humanity.

The Bible teaches us things that we would never have known

unless it was written. The Word of life, the bible, becomes the manual guiding us towards that fulfilled life. Our heavenly Father has revealed His truth to us His children, through His servants, the apostles, and the prophets and this He continues even to the present. The agent for this revelation is the Holy Spirit.

"Now there are diversities of gifts, but the same Spirit...For to one is given by the Spirit the word of wisdom; to another the word of knowledge by the same Spirit; To another faith by the same Spirit; to another the working of miracles; to another prophecy; to another discerning of spirits" (1 Cor.12:4-10). The bible goes on to say and "God hath set some in the church, first apostles, secondarily prophets, thirdly teachers, etc. (1 Cor.12:28).

The Holy Spirit is able to impart to apostles and prophets a special gift for a special purpose. No prophet uttered words that were of his own will but he spoke the word of God as the Holy Spirit gave utterance. It did not require an eloquently speaking man or someone of higher education. Although a prophet may fall short as the common man does, when the Spirit was upon him he was infallible, for his teachings were not his own but that of the Holy Spirit.

Even in today's church we are told to search the Scripture and test His word to see if it is true. How can this be done without relying on human reasoning? Our reliance must be guided through prayers and trust in the Holy Spirit revealing to us what our ordinary eye and mind cannot see and comprehend. We must know that God transcends human reasoning. No man can dictate or predict what it is that God through His Holy Spirit will do. This reminds me of a scripture in the book of Ecclesiastes 7:14-15, "In the day of prosperity be happy, But in the day of adversity consider-God has made the one as well as the other so that man will not discover anything that will be after him." We are ever reminded that He is in control of this universe. The work of God, the Son, and the Holy Spirit is a mystery. If only humanity could accept their limitations by agreeing.

It is the Holy Spirit who gives us the insight into the mysteries and secret knowledge of Him who has called us into this work of the ministry of service, for His glory. There remains a wide gap in the understanding of the Person of the Holy Spirit when compared with the other three religions of Islam, Hinduism and Judaism. To see the Holy Spirit other than the third Person of the Triune is to deny God the Father and the Son.

The person and work of the Holy Spirit is one with the Father and the Son. God the Father is a Spirit as Jesus Christ is of the Father who was incarnate and walked the earth. Without Jesus Christ the indwelling presence of the Spirit would not be. The Holy Spirit has been sent as the Spirit of truth to guide, teach, comfort, counsel, convict, strengthen, witness, glorify, intercede, lead, hear, console, and above all to draw us in the worship to our God.

He is always with us; never you forget that.

Conclusion

I conclude this book with such a humble adulation to Our Almighty God, because all that I am is in Him. Without God, this weight of thought would not have been lifted up. I remain ever so humbled to God for His *call* in my life for service unto His Church. I have written for the purpose of inviting all God's children from the Americas to Africa, Europe, to the Middle East; Asia, to Australia, to know that God is a God who works mysteriously with His creation in unique ways and forms, for His glory. I pray that this book will be used in the seminary walls of academia to help contribute to the lives of those who are in search of the knowledge of God. That they may indeed know that our God is [in many ways]a living God. He desires our adoration of Him always. I also want to encourage those who are *called*, whether in the church or in the teaching academia, to rise tall to their assignment unwavering and uncompromisingly in their defense of our FAITH.

To every church apostle, prophet, evangelist, pastor, teacher, and bishop, it is my hope that we all can continue this journey trusting the one who has *called* us. As the disciples of Jesus Christ we must continue to disciple in every corner we find ourselves for this is our commission.

This book is written for non-believers who are seeking to find their way to know that God is real and that there is no part in our lives that He is not involved in. The message in this book instructs those who have been taught and have accepted that the spiritual things of God are not active in our present time, this is not the case. If only you can surrender and allow Him, you will be directed according to His Will for a better place in this journey called life.

I stated in the preface that the goal for this book is that all will come to the understanding of the truth about the grace of God and to better understand God's *calling* and the *called*. My life story, the works that the LORD is doing in my life, are meant to bring encouragement and enrichment to those who have doubts about God, so that they do not have to doubt anymore but can grow in their personal walk with Christ.

I have written on three major areas, central to our worship to God. Some areas are of deeper theological exposition, some doctrinal, and some from my life experiences. I have shared the Person and the works of the Holy Spirit, the Eucharist or the Lords Supper, and the infant Baptism. I pray that through the grace of God and His inspiration that the Holy Spirit will teach you and bring you clarity in those areas of your struggle.

Through the grace of God I have presented persuasive and purposeful writing and instruction in areas where understanding was lacking, and extended exhortation in other areas that must be confronted. I hope that I have been able to dispel fears, inspire those meandering, and able to edify those who do not want to settle for a lukewarm walk with Jesus, to now be encouraged in strength.

In closing, I pray that you will grow in knowledge and love for the Lord. As you discover the wisdom in His commandments may you be ever so joyful to obey and follow Him all the days of your life. I pray the Lord's divine purpose in your life and mine be done for His glory.

Be blessed in the name of Jesus Christ our Lord.

Amen.

Bibliography

Anderson, Ray S, ed. *The Soul of Ministry*, Westminster John Knox Press, 1997.

Benjamin W. Farley, *Colloquium on Calvin Studies*, Davidson, NC, 1984, 119.

Green, Michael. *I Believe in the HOLY SPIRIT*, William B. Eerdmans Publishing Company, 1975, 2004.

Kelly, J.N.D. *Early Christian Doctrine*, New York, NY: Harper Collins, 1978.

Kelly, J.N.D., *Early Christina Doctrines*, San Francisco: Harper Collins Publishers, 1960.

Moltman, Jurgen. *The Church in the Power of the Spirit*, Minneapolis, MN: First Fortress Press, 1993.

Packer, J.I. *Keep in Step with the Spirit*, Grand Rapids: Baker Books, 1984.

Palmer, Edwin H. *The Holy Spirit: His Person and Ministry*, Baker Book House Company, 1958.

Ray S. Anderson, Lecture ST516 Theology of Christian Community

Ray S.Anderson, *The Soul of Ministry,* Louisville, Ky: Westminster John Knox Press, 1997.

Torrey, R.A. *The Person and Work of the Holy Spirit,* Unites States of America, Whitaker House, 1996.

Walvoord, John F. *The Holy Spirit: A Comprehensive Study of the Person of the Holy Spirit,* Van Kampen Press, 1954.

Wikipedia, *Christian Views on the Holy Spirit,* http://en.wikipedia.org/wiki/Holy_Spirit.

Notes

Notes

About the Author

I currently hold an M.A. in Theology and an M.A. in Theology and Ministry, from Fuller Theological Seminary, Pasadena, C.A. I am pursuing a Ph. D. Degree in Public Policy and Administration-Nonprofit Mgmt & Leadership. I have been sheparding The Bible Church of His Will for over 9 years. I have always had a love for people and a desire for them to get the best out of their lives. My wife and I live in Lomita, California and we have four children between us.